The New Young American Poets

: : : : :

The New Young American Poets

: : : : :

An Anthology

Edited by Kevin Prufer

With a Foreword by Richard Howard

SOUTHERN ILLINOIS UNIVERSITY PRESS : CARBONDALE & EDWARDSVILLE

03   02   01   00   4   3   2   1

Publication partially funded by a subvention grant
from *Pleiades: A Journal of New Writing*

Library of Congress Cataloging-in-Publication Data

The new young American poets : an anthology /
    edited by Kevin Prufer ;
with a foreword by Richard Howard.
          p. cm.
1. American poetry—20th century. I. Prufer, Kevin.
PS615.N46 2000   99-37043
811'.5408—dc21   CIP
ISBN 0-8093-2308-7 (cloth : alk. paper)
ISBN 0-8093-2309-5 (pbk. : alk. paper)

Contents

A Foreword Looking Backwards

In confronting a selection of new poetry by Americans, we would do well to entertain some sentences from Tocqueville (1835) and from Santayana (1900). With these observations in mind, the new reader (for there are, notoriously, new readers as well as new poets in our literary culture) may proceed to a more judicious enjoyment. Here is the Santayana:

> In these latter times, with the prodigious growth of material life in elaboration and of mental life in diffusion, there has supervened . . . a new faith in poetry's absolute power, a kind of return to the inexperience and self-assurance of youth. This new inspiration has made many poets indifferent to traditional disciplines; none of which is seriously to be accepted by them, for the reason, excellent from their own point of view, that no discipline whatever is needed. The memory of ancient disillusions has faded with time. Ignorance of the past has bred contempt for the lessons which the past might teach. Poets prefer to repeat the old experiment without knowing that they repeat it.

And here, seeming to anticipate the consequence is Tocqueville, sixty-five years earlier:

> In democracies it is by no means the case that all who cultivate literature have received a literary education; and most of those who have some tinge of belles-lettres are engaged in professions that only allow them to taste occasionally and by stealth the pleasures of the mind. Accustomed to the struggle, the crosses, and the monotony of practical life, poets require strong and rapid emotions, startling passages, truths or errors brilliant enough to rouse them up and to plunge them at once, as if by violence, into the midst of the subject.

Ours, then, is a generation of poets that knows not the Law, and though the results of such ignorance are often brilliant, and certainly worth our delighted attention, we shall discover that the poetry of our moment, as in the volume that follows, is a literature of desperate measures, dreadful freedoms that only the strongest and most resolute talents can endure. Of course this is what such a culture as ours may want—only the strongest and most resolute talents.

Poetry is already a problematic if not a despised art in what I am calling our moment. Despised because popular. More people are writing what they believe to be poetry, what is even called poetry by their readers, their publishers, their detractors, than ever before in our history—many more are writing poetry than are reading poetry, as you have so often heard. The situation is not a paradox, it is a necessary consequence of our cultural structure. Our academies offer their degrees in unprecedented numbers, for we write, these days, not what we want to keep but what we wish to dispose of. We read only what we value and enjoy. So abject and so absurd has the situation of poetry writing become in our polity—unread though occasionally exhibited, despised though invariably ritualized (as at certain inaugurations)—that not only are we determined to put the poor art out of its misery, we have made it a patriotic duty to do so, declaring a National Poetry Month, for example, to signalize the end of the affair.

A notable stay against confusion is Kevin Prufer's selection. Among the star turns I observe—as a poetry editor myself—that about half the performers have appeared in the periodicals I serve. Others are new to me, or renewed from my own distemper. Noticeable, even evident, almost programmatically clamorous, I think, in the poems presented here is a specifically new accommodation: a dialogue between the private self and the public imagery, between what is *given out* (by the culture, by what we have learned to call the media, though in our society these have ceased to be means and have become ends) and what is *taken in* (by the consumer, by what we so dolefully regard as the separate, even the isolated or sequestered individual). Such a dialogue, in our moment, appears to require the permissive structures of free verse rather than the structures of verse itself (as Tocqueville reminds us). The expression appears to accommodate a larger prose quotient than the poetry of insistently literary contrivance (as Santayana observes). Newspapers and magazines, the movies, television, and now the Internet, the alarmingly identified *Web*—how many of these poems come to terms (and the terms arrived at are the poems) with these promulgated emblems of ourselves!

How many poems are encounters, when they are not conflicts, between recognition and ignorance, between an unacceptable public image and an unsuspected private identity—image prodding identity to account for itself by its very rejection of that image, identity (thus prodded) reacting with more or less resentment, more or less grace! Of course I am not asking a question, I am voicing an exclamation, a wonder, a hope—and I invite the reader to join me in the amazed perscrutation of a current assortment—to discover just how real, how rich, how rewarding our new poetry might be.

Richard Howard

Introduction

Much has been written recently about the dire state of contemporary poetry. Yet, on the surface, these couldn't be more welcoming times for ambitious young poets. Across the nation, more than 250 creative writing programs offer graduate students the chance to concentrate on their craft away from the forty-hour work week. Nine years ago, an article in the May 1991 *Atlantic Monthly* pointed out that by the turn of the century these universities will have granted about twenty thousand advanced degrees in poetry writing. Judging from the reported increase in the number of graduate writing programs in the past few years, those predictions were, if anything, understated.

For those young poets who do not choose the academic path, the world of poetry should seem still friendlier. It has been years since poetry has held mainstream attention the way it does today. MTV advertises "spoken-word" programs in which young writers, the seeming descendants of the beat poets, chant their writing to international audiences. A quick survey of coffee shop bulletin boards in almost any town should encourage anyone interested in performing at poetry slams and open-mike nights or participating in community workshops and reading groups. This year alone at least two nationally distributed films had the poetry slam circuit as their subjects.

In addition, the *1999 Poet's Market* boasts listings for more than eleven hundred nationally circulated magazines and five hundred presses that publish poetry. Despite all the hullabaloo surrounding the cessation of poetry publication by a few high-profile New York publishers, small presses hold close to one hundred poetry book competitions in this country every year, each of which results in the publication of at least one winning collection.

This wealth of resources and outlets, however, can result in confusion for the average reader and frustration for most aspiring writers of poetry. How, after all, can we know where to begin reading, and by what method can a young poet distinguish him or herself?

Each semester, I welcome into my undergraduate creative writing workshop fifteen or twenty aspiring poets. Part of the coursework for the first few weeks involves them going to a library, local bookstore, or World Wide Web site, reading as much poetry published in the last two years as they can, and reporting on their findings. Significantly, most of them return baffled by what they've seen. They find simply too much going on to sum up in a term paper. They have a hard time determining what is innovative and what is imitative and do not know what to say about the seemingly countless movements they encounter—language poetry, new formalism, spoken-word poetry, the New York school. The list, they say, goes on and on.

To make matters worse, there is little in the way of intelligent writing on poetry to help them out. My students—along with many established critics—point out that most book reviewers do not bother reviewing books of poetry. In December of 1997, the *New York Times* listed only six books of poetry among their 136 "Notable Books of Fiction and Poetry." The authors of three of those poetry books were already dead. The 1998 list was not that much more promising. Furthermore, the small amount of press that contemporary poetry does get seems mostly to consist of only glowing reviews, the reviewers perhaps assuming that those less interesting books of poetry will simply fade away if ignored long enough.

So, what may be a superficially inspiring time for those newly emerging poets becomes a trying time for the curious reader or serious writer in search of an audience. This is surely at the root of the many frustrated and angry essays that have appeared in the popular and literary press decrying the state of contemporary poetry and complaining of the youngest generation's failure to live up to the standards of its predecessors. Selected at random—selected even from the most reputable publishers—new American poems imply to the casual reader an age of factionalism, mediocre writing, and the stereotypically boring trained professional poet.

But this is not truly the case. Mixed into this overstimulating if, ultimately, underwhelming poetry scene are many brilliant young writers with strange, exciting, wholly new voices. Some of them have MFAs or teach in creative writing programs, while others spend their days working at the office, teaching high school, or seeing patients, their writing careers pursued in the evenings or on weekends. It has been my goal with this anthology to sort through the piles of new poems by the youngest generation of writers and select forty poets, all born after 1960, who seem to me to be writing unusual, promising poems.

Of course, there exists no easy way of compiling a list of young American poets. For one thing, the field is too huge. For another, part of the idea of an anthology like this is that many of the poets to be considered for inclusion have not yet made themselves well known even to the most avid readers. The majority of those I did finally choose have published just one book, usually with a small press. A handful have only published poems in small literary journals, none offering much in the way of biographical information and many of which are available only by subscription or in large university libraries. And, of course, there are no reference books on the subject.

The selection process for this anthology, therefore, has been as varied as the voices that now make it up. In many cases, a few awkward phone calls determined whether a particularly interesting writer qualified under my age cutoff.

I owe thanks to a number of editors, writers, and teachers who were kind enough to suggest their favorite young poets to me. For obvious reasons, other worthy writers have doubtless escaped my notice.

As I put together a list of the most exciting poets I encountered, I contacted each to discuss which of his or her poems would be included in the anthology. In some cases the poems I'd selected from their bodies of work were acceptable. More often, the poets suggested other, usually newer, poems that I hadn't yet seen. Among their concerns were not only that the anthology include the best of their work but that it also demonstrate, in the allotted few pages, a sense of each individual's range, style, themes, and interests.

I also asked the poets to provide a bit more than the typical two- or three-sentence biographical note that is familiar to any reader of the literary press. Instead, most of the writers have contributed short discussions of their goals, beginnings, and concerns as poets. My hope is that this will not only deepen the readers' understanding of what, exactly, the issues are for the youngest generation of talented poets but will also allow those readers who are interested a more personal way of reading the poems.

There are a number of people who made this project, which at first seemed overwhelming, manageable. Among those who were kind enough to offer suggestions were Hilda Raz at *Prairie Schooner*, Richard Tillinghast, Carl Phillips, Eric Pankey, Susan Ludvigson, R. H. W. Dillard, and Jon Tribble. Many others helped out in different ways. They are Richard Howard, Jennifer Atkinson, Don Bogen, Mary Y. Hallab, R. M. Kinder, and, most of all, John Gehner.

The New Young American Poets

Sherman Alexie

I Would Steal Horses

I would steal horses
for you, if there were any left,
give a dozen of the best
to your father, the auto mechanic

in the small town where you were born
and where he will die in the dark.
I am afraid of his hands, which have
rebuilt more of the small parts

of this world than I ever will.
I would offer my sovereignty, take
every promise as your final lie, the last
point before we start refusing the exact.

I would wrap us both in old blankets
hold every disease tight against our skin.

The Exaggeration of Despair

I open the door

(this Indian girl writes that her brother tried to hang himself
with a belt just two weeks after her other brother did hang himself

and this Indian man tells us that, back in boarding school, five priests
took him into a back room and raped him repeatedly

and this homeless Indian woman begs for quarters, and when I ask
her about the tribe, she says she's horny and bends over in front of me

and this Indian brother dies in a car wreck on the same road
as his older brother, his youngest brother, and the middle brother

and this homeless Indian man is the uncle of an Indian man
who writes for a large metropolitan newspaper, and I know them both

and this Indian child cries when he sits to eat at our table
because he had never known his family to sit at the same table

and this Indian poet shivers beneath the freeway
and begs for enough quarters to buy a pencil and paper

and this fancydancer passes out at the powwow
and wakes up naked, with no memory of the evening, all of his regalia gone

and this is my sister, who waits years for an eagle, receives it
and stores it with our cousins, who then tell her it has disappeared

and this is my father, whose own father died on Okinawa, shot
by a Japanese soldier who must have looked so much like him

and this is my father, whose mother died of tuberculosis
not long after he was born, and so my father must hear coughing ghosts

and this is my grandmother who saw, before the white men came,
three ravens with white necks, and knew our God was going to change)

and invite the wind inside.

Evolution

Buffalo Bill opens a pawn shop on the reservation
right across the border from the liquor store
and he stays open 24 hours a day, 7 days a week

and the Indians come running in with jewelry,
television sets, a VCR, a full-length beaded buckskin outfit
it took Inez Muse 12 years to finish. Buffalo Bill

takes everything the Indians have to offer, keeps it
all catalogued and filed in a storage room. The Indians
pawn their hands, saving the thumbs for last. They pawn

their skeletons, falling endlessly from the skin
and when the last Indian has pawned everything
but his heart, Buffalo Bill takes that for twenty bucks

closes up the pawn shop, paints a new sign over the old,
calls his venture The Museum of Native American Cultures,
charges the Indians five bucks a head to enter.

Theology

the mad barber wants to cut my hair
but he is an atheist

so I am not afraid
if he were religious, say

an insomniac Catholic
or a Muslim with a toothache

I would be terrified
I would have to take him

behind the old warehouse
at Third and Skye

and shoot him twice
once in each eye

Talvikki Ansel

You Don't Know What Happened When You Froze

When buck fever struck,
you stood stiff, unable
to pull the trigger while the herd
crashed past you and
into the woods.

Your cousins—who, one night
when you were all boys, scared
you in the pine grove with a candle
in a cow skull—carried
you to a clearing; they loosened
your hunting vest,
gave you a flask of Jack Daniel's,
and you remembered nothing.

*   *   *

Last night you dreamt of a room—
a room full of fish,
and a swimming pool
where you waded knee-deep
and hauled them all in

except for one, already dead,
a large bluefish wedged
into a corner, its back stiff.

You remember it later: its eye
like a button,
a button on another person's coat.

My Shining Archipelago

A scattering of mottled seeds, spots
of the moon-and-stars melon. A cobalt sea
slips between cliffs and sand-
circled bays. Tug boats, a shadow
of a coasting gull.

*   *   *

On Wona, the dead puppy's ghost
runs into my house, steals
butter from the kitchen table.

When he barks, his voice
is sweet and smooth, a singing drum.

*   *   *

Last week on Luen, the island lecher
made a call, the telephone
became an orange in his hand,
a Seville orange. He has since
devoted his time (most diligently)
to tending the espaliered trees
growing against the garden wall.

*   *   *

On Randherst, the gardeners
wear clogs, they step high and lose
them in the creeks. The shoes float,
painted skiffs, until the village collies
leap and fish them from the eddies.

*   *   *

The general spends hours lobbing
softballs into the limbs
of the catalpa. There are four
schools, but none of them have gym
and this disturbs him. The catalpas
drop chocolate beans all over
the manicured lawns.

*   *   *

The cows on the Winkapins
walk away from the stockyards
and into the fields, they eat
the purple blooming vetch
and watch each other with heavy-
lashed eyes. No one dares chase them.

*   *   *

When it rains for days, the quarries
fill with fresh water. The shells
on the beaches stretch and shine.
Cotton grass, soft as hair on someone
you once touched, grows
into tassels of silk.

*   *   *

When my plane catches fire
above the northern channel marker,
I'll forget to pull the exit
lever, pieces of wing will scatter,

the propeller split into blades
drifting down like maple seeds,
sand-circled, edged and cliffed.

For Want

For want of a flashlight
the stair was lost
mice got into the bins
perched on the cross beams
& ate lemon and mango rinds.

The lid of the teakettle rattled
noodles needed to be broken.
I will get better at this
I promise.

The knuckle-headed squirrel
hangs upside down
scratches mites
wants sunflower seeds,
the coffee wants bite,
more essence of chicory.

To not know what one wants—
I walked it out for weeks in fog
to the tune of
"and binding with briars
my joys and desires"
the motor requires a tune up

the cat wants in, the dog
a scratch behind the ear
the shoe a bear claw sole
the soul a way to throw its gnawed
walnut husk into orbit
to not, no never
rot under leaves.

For want of moisture
the acorn fell, dehisced, dropped
on the roof ping pang.
I had to consult the *I Ching*
and couldn't find it. And

had thrown away the Go Fish cards
which always said only
unhappiness insanity despair.
For want of
none of these prophesies

see it was better not
to have them. Say what you want,
in that bowl on the table
sequins, a bird's nest, hatpins,
a frequent-washer laundry card.

I saw not one other car
all the way the long stretch home,
behind a log truck
leaves and stalks trembling.
Dark, going forward
not wanting a flat tire.

Origin Charm Against Uncertain Injuries

We must read *The Kalevala*, before we forget
birch bark shoes, the bear's long tail
frozen short in the ice,
the shape of the pike, how to bake Rat Bread,
Great Northern Diver. We've forgotten the art

of being silent then sticking a knife
in someone, how to sing the nosy neighbor
into a sea gull. The bee charm, conveyance
charm, a charm for a time of trouble.
We must memorize the captions

in *The Way of the Four Winds*:
"for the herdsman summer passed pleasantly,"
"a white reindeer" and
"Ahku skimming off the fat."
Milkcharm, a charm for coming home,
I whortleberry, I blackberry, I strawberry.

Our Mother has left us for North Farm,
snow smokes off her skis, she does
the push-off to the side, foot-lift
turning corners, like a comet
through hills, the snow-pleated sky.

Remember the field of gold
we weren't allowed to walk in?
Stalks of oil seeds against the blue sky,
shooting rabbits from the side car,
the helmet and goggles. The Sampo—

at North Farm, the mighty Sampo churns out
money, salt and grain. Black-bearded Lemminkainen
wrestles Death's bear, green sparks strike
from his boots. We must read *The Kalevala*,
I whortleberry, I strawberry, I chokeberry.

A charm against worry. I worry, I worry,
I put the charm to the horse, but he doesn't
assume it, carry it away.
"Do not fear wolves," "brew batches
of barley beer." All your worry
all your worry, you must convey away.

Rick Barot

Riffing

The pit of some fruit might be what I'm about
to bite on, speech lapsing to bitterness
that way. Or it might be that a cloud
is paring away from the sun, the sun striking
meaning on something that has to shine.
From a limited meter, Frost says, endless
possibilities for tune. And so I love how
do re mi becomes another nature in my book.
How Tom, Dick, and Harry are all the same
but what I sing about them is different.
Tom's little finger, let's say, or Dick's ear,
or that spare meadow of hair at the small
of Harry's back. I know someone who thinks desire
merely taffies the mind's one want, which is
to be free of want. But I don't live in a bamboo
grove, can't stare at the philosophical cranes
for more than a while. Clean paper only makes me
think of Tom's name repeating itself there.
And the privacy of each face in the subway crowd
suggests that any story *do* might offer
is so distant from what *mi* has to say
that there's no hope for the philosophical.
Someone might be speaking to someone in the dark,
a cigarette the only light between them.
Someone might be crying over a map.
Someone has just about polished a pair of shoes
to his satisfaction. I don't know how dreams
mean, but it's that shoe which often pulls
through to morning, the creases on its snout
like laugh-lines on a face. I think about it
while watching Harry's face waking to *its* lines,
its breath and words. Its *coffee* and *shower*
and *work*. I remember my mother planting roses
as one way the mundane gets brought into

sacredness, though it was simply a thing she liked
to do. Dirt and rain. Leaves and thorns.
Nothing about the fascination with what's
difficult. Nothing about how the soul, in its
limitedness, sings. Just one thing and then
another, Tom says, his tongue here and then here.
Each kiss different and yet somehow the same.
To one rose how many notes can you bring?

Three Amoretti

1. Notes for Bronzino

The mouth to begin with—lightly pursed,
insouciant, as if about to say *insouciant.*
The hair needing cutting, gold, Medicean.
The eyes passing for blue, going green
in good light. Unguardedly private
as sunning cats, hands slack on his lap.
A silver ring on the right fuck-finger;
a necklace of ball bearings under
a t-shirt bleached zinc white. Then, nearly
incommunicable, each iris's black specks;
each cuticle's raw nicks. And the collar
of sunburn on his nape. The freckles
on his shoulders, pale brown and fading—
like the water stains on the bedroom ceiling.

2. On Canal & Broadway

Since you came back I've been all rhymes:
light, sight; teeth, feet; clavicle, navel.
But how to explain that I've lost track
of what it was we came *here* for?
Ginger, bancha tea, or the city's last copy
of *The Mauritius Command?* You stop to tie
your laces and the crowd curves around us,
a river glancing off stones. Couples
carrying string bags of eggplants, newspapers.

Chinese women trailing uncatalogued
bird vocables from their passing chatter.
"Here it is," you say, pointing to a door
whose lettered glass suddenly had us on it.
"Here," you say—word enough for me for now.

3. Battersea Bridge

Like signals indistinctly coming through,
the riverboats are bare blebs of light.
The next bridge is a sketch of bridge,
an arc between posts. Is there a more human
habit than this—to stand here, looking out,
letting our natures yield to all we see
so that the streets, narrowing away
to the world's edges, begin to stand for
our longings? The fog slagging over the city
would stand for our dreaming were we
sleeping, but sign after sign proves
the night OPEN OPEN OPEN. The day's grudges
are on the last trains to the suburbs.
And love, insomniac, burns in the factories.

Portishead Suite

1.

Then I woke up, the shuffle of images still with me. The water near-ice
but bearable. Other figures underneath with me. Leaves moving like
motes in a lightshaft. Goodbye, the kid was saying to the car, the plastic
ball by his feet white as a moon.

Convinced by the dream's exactness, all day I was moved by objects. To
the lime: "Hello, Mambo." To the paperclip: "Hello, Ponge." I thought
of your hand, flat and for once quiet on your chest. Its splay of twenty-
seven bones, complicated as a spider web.

2.

Someone finally had it in them to say that the old lady's hat was now under a seat. Orange, woolen, it had picked up fuzz and a piece of foil wrapper in its slide across the floor. In her backmost teeth, the glint of fillings. Passing lights smeared the train's black windows.

Mercifully soon, the next stop. Looking up from the stairs to the street, I thought Chinese ink-wash for sky. The cold first smell of a chestnut-cart still blocks away. You have to think of it. Chestnut. Coals. The smell that tentative, you have to think of it.

3.

I might stand on the street biding my want. The Flatiron bisects all the sky I can see. There is trash. The legless chair nodding. Wires sprung from the torn gut of plastic. Carpets, endured to ugliness. Dialogue of "I was really torn." "Did you know I waited?" "Did you know?"

One room I remember had a body on a bed that I knew belonged to me but wasn't me. His pants were witless on the floor, his watch was still on his wrist. I could make out the lit numbers. The body lifted with breaths: little, little, little.

4.

Let me tell one truth for a moment. How *landscape* seduces me into putting up the poplars and poppies even before you have told me where we are. The cows are of a color particular to this place. In the background the mountains look like dropped handkerchiefs.

As for *cities*, a friend once described a bus-ride he had to take. Providence, New Haven, White Plains. The bus smelled like pizza, nail polish. And then I was there, too. Knew the orphanage of each bus station he was startled to wake to.

5.

My grandfather had pockets for fried chicken in wax paper, rubber bands, casino chips, and lottery tickets he bought assiduously but whose numbers he never checked for winners. When he died he left behind a roomful of nouns and adjectives.

This life is so fast. I remember coming across that line that goes, "After such knowledge, what forgiveness?" And horrified that the boxes of that knowledge and that forgiveness, as the years went on, would tirelessly fill by themselves.

6.

When I read out loud the part about the antelope going down like a tent, he worries about the tent. Tells a story about the whole afternoon it took to make the tent taut and steady, then his father cauterizing a wound with a pocket knife dipped into campfire embers.

I listen with my head on his stomach. The words gurgle there. There were mosquitoes, but the river was lifeless. He gets hard but continues the story, tries to stay in the two worlds until the last moment. Until, finally, he is subtracted to here.

7.

In the small forest of the city park where we find ourselves talking, sunlight's half a phenomenon of itself, half wind. One shift of the leaves' canopy lights the wedge of your jawline. With another, the glare of eyeglass. I think, I have to try to remember everything.

The light reminds me of the three goldfish I once bought in Chinatown. Feeder fish, the clerk called them, though they grew to the size of small ficus leaves. They lived years even on the barest care. At night I stared at them, their movements small cursives in the dark.

Paul Beatty

That's Not in My Job Description

despite that i overslept
and set a guinness book world record for coming in late
its still time for me to take my 15 minute break

pull off my sweater vest
talking shit

cross my sneakers on the desk
threaten to call my union rep
if these fools

        dont stop lookin at me crazy
        whisperin lazy
        under their breath

but during my siesta
i eavesdrop on societys best

        imagine im a distinguished ethnographer

on the black pbs
talking with a british lip
in front of a bookshelf

welcome to *In Search of*
today we pursue The Elusive True Nature of Whitey

        notice as
        our cameras
        zoom in on

a pin-striped pack of business school well groomed brooks brother smoothies
encamped around a water cooler jostling for room in their natural habitat
wiping dunkin donut crumbs off their jackets and engaged in debates
on hot topics
such as:

     nuclear waste   the china syndrome
     alternative methods of heating their homes
                    and right before

        the herd start to roam

     the menfolk take part in the ritual
     shooting of the styrofoam cups into the trash basket

if they make it
they dance around like
they just saved the world

headin my way
lookin for some dap

so i try to look busy
which im good at

start rustlin charts
construct some new paper clip art
chew on a pen cap as if im seriously studying my messenger map

hmmmm   did you know that main street runs perpendicular to beech
             and parallel with elm for exactly 1 and seven/eighteenths of
               a mile
             before it intersects with west crest
             well blow me down

i aint got time to mope
worryin aloud about
how imma cope wid radioactive isotopes and mushroom clouds

     when its me myself

thats about to explode

an overloaded low level gung-ho ah-so nigro richshaw coolie
the company dr. doolittles thought they knew me
i talk to the animals como se llama   push-me-pull-me

bowin n kowtowin
eatin crow
holdin my tongue
hands clung so tightly to the bottom rung
cant even reach for the glass ceiling

        my feet planted in corporate dung

    growing roots
          in the ground zero
               terra firma
         of affirmative
  daily inaction

         copy xerox mop remember the blue ones go on top
         shred fedex the checks press the red button next
         fax wax collapse the green mail sacks go to jack

right after i put my year-end evaluation
in the management trainee mailbox

one of them fresh out of college cookie cutter fuckers
invites me to meet the buddies for drinks at mcgillicuddy's

i only wanted a nine to five
that classified didn't say noting bout havin to socialize

now this wage slave
is t-minus nine heinekens from critical mass

    me and a few hoogie white democrats
    drinking after work rolling rocks
    smoking marlboros out the box

all you can do is wait for the chain reaction show of ass

when one of em
looks me in the eye

      and decides
           to say something to the colored guy

its
all systems go
the white folks start actin like they know

      hey bro er uh bro-ham
      i happen to be a big rap fan
      went to see ice cube and michel'le
      at the hollywood palladium
      and i was the only white person in the place
      aint i soul brother

there must have been another workshop on how to handle your support staff
which in this craft is a euphemism for niggers n spics

itsa trip
watching a one-sided will to unite

if i could get a word in edgewise i wouldnt
                       since im with my boss
                       and dont want to get fired
          all i can do is sigh
                     too chicken to pay the price

as they get excited
giddy from overexercising their rights

my dad owns a liquor store in the inner city so i know how you feel

ive read toni morrisons beloved twice
and even though i still didnt get it the second time shes just so real

i believe that spike is truly five for five
no no you dont understand   i really want to be like mike

or maybe a harlem globetrotter
its my dream to send my daughter to spelman
where can she get a checkup for sickle cell
whats the name of your hair gel/pomade
do you use a depilatory when you shave
how can i join the crips
just *what is hip*
i know its after the fact but i dont think king shouldve called for calm
i wanna be a minister in the nation of islam
isnt so and so an uncle tom

when theyre through
they pat themselves on the back
and quote jesse jackson

we have to start on the front end of head start and day care
not on the back end of prison and welfare

keepin hope alive
i buy the next round

wonderin how it would sound if i changed my name to skip
placed a mike tyson kingsized if i ruled to world chip on my shoulder
went to a joint full of rednecks
put my elbows on the bar cleared my throat and said

becks
then id go into my show

did you know i was elected to the senate inna landslide
and i was the only colored man there without a rag in my hand for
polishin brass or shining shoes

or

at last weeks tractor pull i was the only spear chukker
drivin monster pick-ups over a bunch of crushed oldsmobiles

or

i sailed in the americas cup

or

i went to the university of vermont   and rowed crew

or

i grew up in a two room shack in the appalachian mountains picked myself up
by the shitkickers went door to door selling berlitz and scripture moved to
utah sang soprano in the mormon tabernacle choir married into the osmonds
and now i spend my weekends smokin pot with donnie and marie reading back
issues of teen beat magazine

or

im included in the canon
im a cardinal in the vatican
im the highest paid player on the boston red sox
i own IBM stock
i play nazi punk rock
i drink coors extra gold by the case
i can say puke with a straight face
i have a seat on wall street
im an LL bean catalogue model
my art is in the metropolitan
i had a major part in a woody allen movie
and i do the broadway casting for tommy tune

but i wouldnt give a shit about nuna dis
if i could just say   im a nigger who has enough room

Erin Belieu

Nocturne: My Sister Life

I

Honeysuckles tap soil
        almost anywhere, junkyard
shrubs, able-rooted, attaching
        through rock or sand. From
Evanston to Omaha, their red fish
        roe berries border plots
of zoysia, buffalo, the family portion.
        Lilacs go slowly, their old lady wigs
curling to beige crust; roses might
        develop, but die in extreme weather.
Depend on the honeysuckle
        to maintain where others falter . . .

II

*You were never afraid of the dark, never afraid of each object resolving itself,
vanishing into night's good sleeve, benign magic the world performed for you at
sundown. You admired the young shepherdess tending sheep at the base of your
lamp, coaxing her flock into evening's invisible pen. You wanted the world quiet.
Even then, you looked forward to all things shutting their many mouths, interim in
the revolving puzzle of light.*

III

Scent of an eighth-grader's
        cologne, they strong-arm other shrubs,
are used primarily for husbandry.
        Honeysuckles provide cheap
borders, hide chain-link fences.

Won't tuck behind your ear, attract
bees bad as marigolds and stand
        awkwardly in floral arrangements.
While not poisonous, the jellied
        berries can be semitoxic. Some
might not resist the urge to eat them,
        even after being warned against it . . .

IV

Lying in your twin bed, where cartoon figures stare out from the comforter with
their medicated expressions, you realize that you're dying, death includes you.
Distant relatives, rodents, and now, suddenly, you. This is the same day you're
surprised by a nest of wasps hidden in the neighbors' swing set, their jet bodies
burrowing inside your clothes, stinging you between the shoulder blades, one welt
bubbling inside your lower lip. Imagine everything dead: your older brother,
somewhere in the house, closer to it. Your parents in the den, crunch of the ice
bucket as your father fixes his Manhattan (gold anesthesia, issued to the heart),
closer still.

V

When stands of honeysuckle
        fade, they reach for the ground,
their nippled flowers pulling close
        to the center of each bush.
Birds abandon old nests
        laid open inside the dying
grove. Eventually the shrubs
        must be stumped, hacked off
below the waist and extracted.
        Do not be shocked by their roots,
how far the honeysuckles' reach is . . .

VI

Now you lie down queen-sized, new husband beside you, paying rent in his dreams. Yesterday, he tells you, you woke with two questions: Needle? Needle? Who knows, the way you sleep, you might as well be drowning. The dragonfly stuck in a knick-knack's liquid glass. Sometimes you drive a yellow Karmann Ghia through your dream-scapes, clown-mobile with transparent, cardboard windows. Through shopping malls, bordellos, your cousins' basement, you always ferry a passenger. Wake and something else is waking: your familiars at the window, stalking what moves on the ledge.

A Sleeping Man Must Be Awakened to Be Killed

All afternoon I thought the decision must fall
between two abstractions:

what is merciful
versus
what is honorable;

whether to wake the sleeping man before
they kill him, or not. I confess

my interest wasn't
noble. The morning news
unfolded details which,

unfortunately, fascinate: a tiny camera hidden
in a teapot he'd requested,

by which they saw him count
his many sticks of dynamite,
booby-trap the entryways

then fall into an agitated sleep; the dilemma
of children as hostages. What got to me, finally,

was how young the kids were,
only three and four. I pictured
them in a yellow schoolroom,

looking lost, helplessly cranky,
a piano on wheels in one corner.

This day passes. We make dinner,
love; you escape into your own dreams.
It occurs to me, now studying your shut-

eyed flutters, your left hand gripping and releasing
the humid sheet, that what was planned

is practical, must be, directed
by those with practical concerns.
I wonder what they are? I wonder

who decides to wake the sleeping man, maybe dreaming,
maybe lost in the white space between dreams.

What reason to shake him back to where he's gotten
now: this yellow schoolroom, a piano on
wheels? I watch you sleep. You don't answer.

Legend of the Albino Farm

Omaha, Nebraska

They do not sleep nights
but stand between

rows of glowing corn and
cabbages grown on acres past

the edge of the city.
Surrendered flags,

their nightgowns furl and
unfurl around their legs.

Only women could be this
white. Like mules,

they are sterile,
and it appears that

their mouths are always
open. Because they are thin

as weeds, the albinos
look hungry. If you drive out

to the farm, tree branches will
point the way. No map will show

where, no phone is listed.
It will seem that the moon, plump

above their shoulders, is constant,
orange as harvest all year

long. We say, when a mother
gives birth to an albino girl,

she feigns sleep after
labor while an Asian

man steals in, spirits
the pale baby away.

Rondeau at the Train Stop

It bothers me: the genital smell of the bay
drifting toward me on the T stop, the train
circling the city like a dingy, year-round
Christmas display. The Puritans were right! Sin
is everywhere in Massachusetts, hell-bound

in the population. It bothers me
because it's summer now and sticky—no rain
to cool things down; heat like a wound
that will not close. Too hot, these shameful
percolations of the body that bloom
between strangers on a train. It bothers me

now that I'm alone and singles foam
around the city, bothered by the lather, the rings
of sweat. Know this bay's a watery animal, hind-end
perpetually raised: a wanting posture, pain
so apparent, wanting so much that it bothers me.

Rafael Campo

What the Body Told

Not long ago, I studied medicine.
It was terrible, what the body told.
I'd look inside another person's mouth
And see the desolation of the world.
I'd see his genitals and think of sin.

Because my body speaks the stranger's language,
I've never understood those nods and stares.
My parents held me in their arms, and still
I think I've disappointed them; they care
And stare, they nod, they make their pilgrimage

To somewhere distant in my heart, they cry.
I look inside their other-person's mouths
And see the sleek interior of souls.
It's warm and red in there—like love, with teeth.
I've studied medicine until I cried

All night. Through certain books, a truth unfolds.
Anatomy and physiology,
The tiny sensing organs of the tongue—
Each nameless cell contributing its needs.
It was fabulous, what the body told.

The Battle Hymn of the Republic

Defending you, my country, hurts
My eyes. I see the drums, the glory,
The marching through the gory
Unthinkable mud of soldier's guts

And opened hearts: I want to serve.
I join the military,
Somehow knowing that I'll never marry.
The barracks' silence as I shave

Is secretive and full of cocks.
I think to myself, What if I'm a queer,
What if too many years
Go by and then my brain unlocks-

The days seem uniformed,
Crisp salutes in all the trees;
A sandstorm buries the casualties
Of a war. What if I were born

This way, I think to myself,
What if I were dead,
An enemy bullet in my head?
I see the oil burning in the Gulf,

Which hurts my eyes. My sergeant cries.
Now he's a real man—
I sucked his cock behind a van
In the Presidio, beneath a sky

So full of orange clouds
I thought I was in love.
I think to myself, What have
I become? I lose myself in the crowds

Of the Castro, the months go by
And suddenly they want to lift the ban.
I don't think they can.
I still want to die

My death of honor, I want to die
Defending values I don't understand;
The men I see walking hand in hand
Bring this love song to my mind.

Asylum

Demented underneath the moon, I watch
The street conduct electric sparks tonight,
These cars, their headlights, energy in flight—

Skyscrapers precarious as men in heels.
This night, it seems more glamorous than real.
Demented underneath the moon, around

Another corner, ten men beat the pan
Of shiny, pooling blood another man
Has made for them, his whole life's work: these men

Identified another queer. The moon
Demented underneath the fleeting stars,
Demented, shining on the speeding cars,

Dissolves upon my tongue. It tastes like force.
It tastes like blood, saliva, teeth. I'd curse,
But I'm demented. Underneath the moon,

The moonlight makes perfection out of me.
The men are beating on their drum. Their drums
Are poverty and ignorance, so painfully

Made lucid. Once, I really saw the moon.
It hurt. And underneath it all the world
Was busy, furious, bent to the loom.

My Childhood in Another Part of the World

The world was quiet then.
A child was playing dead,
Avoiding being immunized.
I lived in Venezuela when

Democracies could kill.
A child was turning red,
Beneath a sun he understood
Was angry. Miracle

Of miracles, the world
Was children taking guns
Away from soldiers—run!
Through streets like mental wards.

The world confused me then.
A child was clenching in
His fist the Ritalin
He would not take. In mine,

I shielded a secret thing:
A large, bright-emerald beetle.
Revealed, it would startle
Adults, who thought it menacing.

My childhood, my childhood,
Returning to me. I was
Too dumb to be unwise,
Too young to be so unafraid.

Towards Curing AIDS

I slap on latex gloves before I put
My hands inside the wound. A hypocrite
Across the room complains that it's her right
To walk away—to walk away's her right
As a physician. Lapidary, fine,
My patient's eyes are overhearing her.
He doesn't wince. His corner bed inters
Him even now, as she does: he hasn't died
But he will. The right to treatment medicine
Denied is all the hollows here: along
His arms, the hungry grooves between the bones

Of ribs. As if her surgeon's thread through skin—
The rite of obligation overdue—
Could save him now. I close the wound. The drain
Is repositioned. Needles in his veins,
I leave him pleading. There's too much to do.

Nick Carbó

"When the grain is golden and the wind is chilly, then it is the time to harvest"

Leron-leron sinta, umakyat sa papaya
Dala-dala'y buslo', sisidlan ng bunga

In a dusty village in Cagayan Valley,
Ramon and his father were planting rice when soldiers

appeared on their farm. They questioned his father,
had he seen any communist rebels recently

in the area, and when he did not give them
a good enough answer, they beat him with the blunt ends

of their rifles, shot him as he was lying
on the ground. Ramon snuck away but remained hidden

in nearby bushes, to witness the soldiers
laugh out loud as they chopped his father's shaking body—

"they first removed his penis, then cut below
the knees, then the ankles, then the elbows, then the neck."

Leron-leron sinta, umakyat sa papaya
Dala-dala'y buslo', sisidlan ng bunga

After dusk Ramon ran home to his mother
and younger brother. She feared the soldiers would soon knock

---

This poem is derived from events retold by the director of the Children's Rehabilitation Center in Manila in an interview in Joseph Collins, ed., *The Philippines: Fire on the Rim*, San Francisco: The Institute for Food and Development Policy, 1989 (296–99). The first two lines are from a Filipino folk song children sing while they are playing.

on their door, so she took her sons deep inside
the muddy jungle of the Sierra Madre mountains.

After about four weeks, she sent Ramon to buy
rice, some fish, and a few canned goods. The sun was heavy,

the road to the village kept stretching further,
and his legs felt weak, so Ramon boarded a jeepney

to take him to the market on Luna street.
A soldier recognized him at a military

checkpoint and he pointed his gun at Ramon,
yelled at him to step out with his hands up in the air.

Leron-leron sinta, umakyat sa papaya
Dala-dala'y buslo', sisidlan ng bunga

No questions were asked. Ramon told us the most
painful torture he endured was when the soldiers joined

two blocks of wood and used the weapon to hit
him directly on the ears, over and over

until he bled. He doesn't remember how
he escaped but he found himself wandering around

the countryside for many days, eating grass,
guava leaves, bamboo shoots, and bananas to survive.

Leron-leron sinta, umakyat sa papaya
Dala-dala'y buslo', sisidlan ng bunga

Here at the Children's Rehabilitation
Center, Ramon made friends, played with the other children,

started to learn how to write. He asked questions
about his mother and younger brother, he wanted

to know when he could return to his village
to harvest their rice fields. He said it was important

to go home because "when the grain is golden
and the wind is chilly, then it is the time to harvest."

After four months, we learned that Ramon's mother
was probably dead. "Where's the body? I want to see

the body, I want to bury my mother."
I told him we didn't know where the body was, but we

would try to find it. After a long silence,
he finally went to his room. Then I followed him

upstairs, found him hunched over the bathroom sink
washing his red face again and again and again.

Leron-leron sinta, umakyat sa papaya
Dala-dala'y buslo', sisidlan ng bunga

Ramon is still with us, his friends have brought him
out of his shell, he has learned how to speak Tagalog,

and he is beginning to read. Ramon dreams
about going home. He writes letters to his younger

brother even though we tell him he is still
missing. We collect those letters he writes every day.

He tells his younger brother, "If you come here,
you will have many good friends to play with, eat plenty

of food, and these nice people will let us stay
here in Manila, but maybe I will go home first

and see what's happened to our family farm."
He then writes, "Do you know that your mother is now dead?"

Little Brown Brother

I've always wanted to play the part
of that puckish pubescent Filipino boy

in those John Wayne Pacific-War movies.
Pepe, Jose, or Juanito would be smiling,

bare-chested, and eager to please
for most of the steamy jungle scenes.

I'd be the one who would cross
the Japanese lines and ask for tanks,

air support, or more men. I'd miraculously
make it back to the town where John Wayne

is holding his position against the enemy
with his Thompson machine gun. As a reward,

he'd rub that big white hand on my head,
and he'd promise to let me clean

his Tommy gun by the end of the night. But
then, a Betty Grable look-alike love

interest would divert him by sobbing
into his shoulder, saying how awfully scared

she is about what the "Japs" would do
to her if she were captured. In one swift

motion, John Wayne would sweep her off
her feet to calm her fears inside his private quarters.

Because of my Hollywood ability
to be anywhere, I'd be under the bed

watching the woman roll down her stockings
as my American hero unbuckles his belt.

I'd feel the bottom of the bed bounce off my chest
as small-arms fire explodes outside the walls.

The Filipino Politician

When he finds his wife in bed with another man—

The conservative politician feels an ache in his stomach,
        remembers the *longanisa* and the *tapa* he had for breakfast.
He doesn't know whether to get the doctor or Cardinal Sin
        on the phone. He calls one of his bodyguards, tells him
to shoot the man and then his wife. He takes his .38 magnum
        from his briefcase, shoots his bodyguard in the back.

The liberal politician pours himself a glass of Courvoisier,
        remembers a passage from an Anais Nin story.
He is suddenly the one they call the *Basque*. He removes
        his Dior tie, his Armani shirt, his Calvin Klein boxer shorts.
He puts on a black beret, whispers *tres jolie, tres jolie,*
        que bonito, muy grande my petite amor. He joins them
in bed, begins his caresses on the man's calves,
        kisses his way up the man's thighs.

The communist politician does not call his wife a *puta*,
        nor does he challenge the man to a duel with *balison* knives.
He stays calm, takes out a book of poems by Mao Tse Tung.
        Inspired, he decides to advance the Revolution.
He takes a taxi to Roxas Boulevard and begins to curse
        and throw rocks at the American Embassy.

Votive Candles

for Denise

I tell my mother my girlfriend is a good Catholic girl—
every Wednesday, she lights electric votive candles
in Our Lady of Guadalupe Church on 14th Street.

She prays that I don't leave her, that no one
mugs me on the way home, that the electricity used
to light the candles doesn't waste energy

and increase our country's dependence on foreign oil.
She has pictures of the Virgin Mary on the wall
in the hallway to her studio. Below these pictures

is a rack of plastic, brass, and pewter jewelry.
She says that the Virgin protects her,
that her apartment was robbed twelve times

and they never stole her earrings, bracelets,
and necklaces. She writes about her desire
for Catholic-school girls to become

popes or presidents. She hopes someday a woman
will run the Vatican. My mother asks me if my girlfriend
has ever been to confession. I tell her that she has had

the first and a few others, but what really matters
is that she writes confessional poetry,
that the whole world can be the judge of her sins,

mortal or venial. My mother says she'll pray for us,
light two real candles in the chapel
for the Perpetual Help of Jesus.

Joshua Clover

The map room

We moved into a house with 6 rooms: the Bedroom,
the Map Room, the Vegas Room, Cities
in the Flood Plains, the West, & the Room Which Contains All
of Mexico. We honeymooned in the Vegas Room where
lounge acts wasted our precious time. Then there was the junta's
high command, sick dogs of the Map Room, heel
prints everywhere, pushing model armies into the unfurnished
West. At night: stories of their abandoned homes in the Cities
in the Flood Plains, how they had loved each other
mercilessly, in rusting cars, until the drive-in went under.
From the Bedroom we called the decorator & demanded
a figurehead . . . the one true diva to be had
in All of Mexico: Maria Felix [star of *The Devourer*, star
of *The Lady General*]. Nightly in Vegas, "It's Not Unusual"
or the Sex Pistols medley. Nothing ever comes back
from the West, it's a one-way door, a one-shot deal, —
the one room we never slept in together. My wife
wants to rename it the Ugly Truth. I love my wife for her
wonderful, light, creamy, highly reflective skin;
if there's an illumination from the submerged Cities,
that's her. She suspects me of certain acts involving Maria Felix,
the gambling debts mount . . . but when she sends the junta off to Bed
we rendezvous in the Map Room & sprawl across the New World
with our heads to the West. I sing her romantic melodies from the Room
Which Contains All of Mexico, tunes which keep arriving
like heaven, in waves of raw data, & though I wrote
none of the songs myself & can't pronounce them, these are my greatest hits.

El periférico, or sleep

A man throws ten thousand shovels of gravel at a window screen
propped upside a wheelbarrow so only the powder
passes into the wheelbarrow and the gray rocks fall to the ground.

You musta died once to live like this.
Yeah he says I died once and I had lost my ear
so I was looking for it in a field and the stars were like a seiner's net
and then they were like a system of nerves
and then they were like a sieve I came through
that right back into this country and got a job and married
the woman the first two things
she said to me in that fiery field holding in her hands
my ear were how this country now is full
only of pilgrims and residue and her name is Beatriz ending
like light ends with a *z*.

"An archive of confessions, a genealogy of confessions"

Now the summer air exerts its syrupy drag on the half-dark
City under the strict surveillance of quotation marks.

The citizens with their cockades and free will drift off
From the magnet of work to the terrible magnet of love.

In the far suburbs crenellated of Cartesian yards and gin
The tribe of mothers calls the tribe of children in

Across the bluing evening. It's the hour things get
To be excellently pointless, like describing the alphabet.

Yikes. It's fine to be here with you watching the great events
Without taking part, clinking our ice as they advance

Yet remain distant. Like the baker always about to understand
Idly sweeping up that he is the recurrence of Napoleon

In a baker's life, always interrupted by the familiar notes
Of a childish song, "no more sleepy dreaming," we float

Casually on the surface of the day, staring at the bottom,
Jotting in our daybooks, how beautiful, the armies of autumn.

"Alas, that is the name of our town; I have been concealing it all this time"

The stars were strange lightbulbs, the moon was half
A spectacle, they wandered into the vestibule
Of evening as the fat clouds fainted away,
Looking a little confused like one who arrives
Just a few minutes late for dinner to find flowers
Overgrowing the good silver, blossoms of baby yellow
And baby blue. Quel drag. Two boys climbed
Arm in arm toward the observatory, panting
And laughing on the long terraced steps. People ran
Up past the small balcony houses just to turn
And run down again, paying brief attention
To the many tastes of the balconistas, the hanging
Plants and decorations, that white facade ragged
With leftover wedding festoons. A woman
Walked backward up the stairs, leaving the library
To the rats and the readers, modest mice,
And each person on the hill who noticed her
Daydreamy ascent recalled how much they enjoyed
Watching movies in reverse, the milk pouring upward
Into a blue-rimmed glass, into order, the undoing action
Of the sublime. Though barely evening it felt late
In the something, some larger shape which could not
Be seen though it pressed against you and seemed
To hum, a diversionary tune of so few notes
Repeated so indifferently it's hardly a tune at all,
Except what else could you call it? Who knows,
You answered, knowing most of the brilliant motion
To be already taken, the vast and whirling
Subterranean armature just now beginning
To wind down in earnest, and we have yet to invent
Anything so pure as the guillotine, an instrument
Known also as the little window. But what shall
We hope to see there? The marriage of the beautiful
And the trivial? That the sky finally
Emptied of clouds must now say a new thing?

Nicole Cooley

Mary Warren's Sampler

You were a little while ago an Afflicted person, now you are an Afflicter:
How comes this to pass?

—Judge Hathorne and Judge Corwin

Reversible Stitches: my mother and I leaned over a single piece of English linen—I want her smooth white hands not my master's fingers pinching the skin along my backbone voice breathing *Mary*—Single Satin Stitch—I stand before the court and I say *I am sorry for it I am sorry* and the girls shut their eyes—at home he struck my arm I hid behind the spinning wheel I hid from him— Chain Stitch—I gripped my mother's wrist her cold hand folded on the sheet of the bed we shared—*I will tell I will tell*—he said he'd thrash the Devil out of me he said he'd drown me in the creek behind the barn—Lace Filling Stitch— Mother's pattern book open on my lap I copied *A Noble and Generous Fear Proceeds From Love* in silk thread—I licked my finger my black spit leaked onto the page—the girls at any moment will fall down together hands set at their throats to show I am a witch—My master's iron tongs could burn me out of my fit—Fishbone Stitch—my mother bent over the cloth head bowed to tie each small knot I touched her gleaming hair—In the court I bite my lips and whisper the lesson *Fear Proceeds From Love Love Is Fear*—Buttonhole Stitch—he told me *If you are Afflicted I wish you were more Afflicted*—My fingers blackened bread and butter when I set his table and I screamed—Backstitch to the Past—to the edge of Eve's body we arranged at the sampler's border—to Fear to the marks along my arm his fingers made like stitches—he called me his *Jade* his body crushing mine until—Darning Stitch Cross Stitch Loop Stitch—*I will tell I will tell It was the Devil's book my master Proctor brought me*—as witness my hand Mary Warren

Publick Fast on Account of the Afflicted: March 31, 1692

If we eat, we choke. Bread wedges in our throats.
Peas are pins

that prick the tongue. Our mothers' milk burns our lungs
as if we're drowning.

We gag and gag until the Reverend vows to cure this village:
together, every family

will fast and pray to drive the witches from our land.
In the meeting house,

the Sacrament cracks on the black plate. The Reverend reads.
Dear Lord, Receive

Our Souls. Take Our Mortal Bodies. Save These Afflicted.
We wait, shoulder

to shoulder, lean together in the pew like sisters. *Abigail.*
Mary. Mercy. Elizabeth.

Our secret circles us, keeping us safe. The whitewashed walls
block out the sun,

yet we four see beyond the visible—We dream
the witches' Black Mass Meal:

milk sweetened with spit. Finger bones folded under the skin
of a pudding.

Urine-drizzled gruel. We agree: the witches tear bread as if
it were girls' flesh.

Abigail. Mary. Mercy. Elizabeth. As if the bread were our bodies.
We'll tell the story.

We'll choke, hold our throats closed with our breath, until
the women disappear.

The Reverend doesn't know, but our love fills us, links us
like a line of paper dolls.

The candles burn and burn and burn. Against the other women,
we are one body.

The Mother: Dorcas Good

> *these swooning fits were . . . nothing else*
> *but what they call the mother.*
> —Sir Thomas Brown, *A Tryal of Witches*
> *of the Assizes Held at Bury St. Edmunds*, 1682

Snow fills the fields like milk.
Inside the Meeting House I wait on the communion table.
I unbutton my muslin dress while the Reverend reads

To the Marshall of Essex or his Deputy:
You are in their Magistrates names hereby required
to bring before us Dorcus Good.

I am four years old. My dress drops from my body.
The three girls circle, calling
the mother, the mother, holding their throats with their hands.

I close my eyes: I'm outside in the snow,
standing in the harbor's dark throat we followed
here, to the New Jerusalem.

Or I'm with my mother in Ipswich Jail.

The Reverend holds a candle close
to each girl's wrist, to the teeth marks in a row,
like tiny stitches, they say are mine.

                    In jail, my mother pulls
me into her lap, cradles my head against her chest
as my mouth reaches for her nipple.

Here is the Devil's Mark, the Reverend raises
my hand for all to see. A small red bite.
A perfect circle on my palm.

Did a yellow bird suck here between your fingers?

                    I close my eyes
and the bird spreads its wings
on my mother's shoulders, hiding us, keeping us safe.

Now Child, repeat the prayer.
Up on the table, my arms stretched out:
Our Father, Who Art in Heaven, Hallowed Be Thy Name.

I could be a bird. The girls still circle.
When I look at them they fall against each other
like the rag dolls my mother arranged on my bed at home.

                  I want to be invisible.
I want to go back to my mother's body.

Branches snap off the black trees on Gallows Hill.
Ice cracks on the roof of the jail.
This girl is a witch. The men in the front pew nod.

The girls let go of their throats.
Does my mother sleep in jail alone? I want to call to her.
I can't. My body stands straight and still on the examining table,

                                    my voice torn out—

John Winthrop, "Reasons to be Considered for . . . the Intended Plantation in New England," 1629

> *Increase and multiply, replenish the earth and subdue it.*
> —Genesis 1:28

Who is the author of Disaster?
>> For an answer, read
>>> The Book of Nature or
>>>> a woman's face.

the whole earth is the Lord's garden

Who will guide us
>> out of Egypt, over the Red Sea,
>>> the color of shame,
>>>> into the New Jerusalem?

this land grows weary of her inhabitants

England was the lover
>> you must leave behind,
>>> the New World is your wife,
>>>> her body the City on the Hill.

the church hath no place left to fly but into the wilderness

Split the trees at the root,
>> slash the salt grass to clear
>>> a long road to the future.
>>>> Lock your wife in the house.

Keep yourself safe.
Remember that the Invisible World is full of women.

Denise Duhamel

Sex with a Famous Poet

I had sex with a famous poet last night
and when I rolled over and found myself beside him I shuddered
because I was married to someone else,
because I wasn't supposed to have been drinking,
because I was in a fancy hotel room
I didn't recognize. I would have told you
right off this was a dream, but recently
a friend told me, *write about a dream,*
lose a reader and I didn't want to lose you
right away. I wanted you to hear
that I didn't even like the poet in the dream, that he has
four kids, the youngest one my age, and I find him
rather unattractive, that I only met him once,
that is, in real life, and that was in a large group
in which I barely spoke up. He disgusted me
with his disparaging remarks about women.
He even used the word "Jap"
which I took as a direct insult to my husband who's Asian.
When we were first dating, I told him
"You were talking in your sleep last night
and I listened, just to make sure you didn't
call out anyone else's name." My future-husband said
that he couldn't be held responsible for his subconscious,
which worried me, which made me think his dreams
were full of blond vixens in rabbit-fur bikinis,
but he said no, he dreamt mostly of boulders
and the ocean and volcanoes, dangerous weather
he witnessed but could do nothing to stop.
And I said, "I dream only of you,"
which was romantic and silly and untrue.
But I never thought I'd dream of another man—
my husband and I hadn't even had a fight,
my head tucked sweetly in his armpit, my arm
around his belly, which lifted up and down

all night, gently like water in a lake.
If I passed that famous poet on the street,
he would walk by, famous in his sunglasses
and blazer with the suede patches at the elbows,
without so much as a glance in my direction.
I know you're probably curious about who the poet is,
so I should tell you the clues I've left aren't
accurate, that I've disguised his identity,
that you shouldn't guess *I bet it's him* . . .
because you'll never guess correctly
and even if you do, I won't tell you that you have.
I wouldn't want to embarrass a stranger
who is, after all, probably a nice person,
who was probably just having a bad day when I met him,
who is probably growing a little tired of his fame—
which my husband and I perceive as enormous,
but how much fame can an American poet
really have, let's say, compared to a rock star
or film director of equal talent? Not that much,
and the famous poet knows it, knows he's not
truly given his due. Knows that many
of these young poets tugging on his sleeve
are only pretending to have read all his books.
But he smiles anyway, tries to be helpful.
I mean, this poet has to have some redeeming qualities, right?
For instance, he writes a mean iambic.
Otherwise, what was I doing in his arms.

Ego

I just didn't get it—
even with the teacher holding an orange (the earth) in one hand
and a lemon (the moon) in the other,
her favorite student (the sun) standing behind her with a flashlight.
I just couldn't grasp it—
this whole citrus universe, these bumpy planets revolving so slowly
no one could even see themselves moving.
I used to think if I could only concentrate hard enough

I could be the one person to feel what no one else could,
sense a small tug from the ground, a sky shift, the earth changing gears.
Even though I was only one mini-speck on a speck,
even though I was merely a pinprick in one goosebump on the orange,
I was sure then I was the most specially perceptive, perceptively sensitive.
I was sure then my mother was the only mother to snap,
"The world doesn't revolve around you!"
The earth was fragile and mostly water,
just the way the orange was mostly water if you peeled it,
just the way I was mostly water if you peeled me.
Looking back on that third grade science demonstration,
I can understand why some people gave up on fame or religion or cures—
especially people who have an understanding
of the excruciating crawl of the world,
who have a well-developed sense of spatial reasoning
and the tininess that it is to be one of us.
But not me—even now I wouldn't mind being god, the force
who spins the planets the way I spin a globe, a basketball, a yoyo.
I wouldn't mind being that teacher who chooses the fruit,
or that favorite kid who gives the moon its glow.

I'm Dealing with My Pain

He's about 300 pounds and knows martial arts, boxing and wrestling—both the real and the fake kind. So I never know when I'm thrown to the ground or hurled against the ropes of a boxing ring fence (who can guess when he'll surprise me with a punch next?) if the ache in my back is real or cartoon, if my bruises will stay or wash off like kiddie tattoos.

Pain is a sneak and a cheat. He loves to eat unhealthy foods (scrapple, greasy gravy, Little Debbie Snacks). Not only that—I think he smokes. I can smell it on his breath, all fire and ash, when he pins me to my bed without asking. He's hefty and invisible and likes to strike in the dark so that even my magnifying glass and double locks are useless. Sometimes I call him Sumo, the Devil, or any member of my family. He's a changeling and a scam. His footprints are the ones that make cracks in the sidewalk.

Pain first introduced himself as a sadist. I was confused at the time. He said he was seduced by the blue of my wrist, the soft hollow at the center of my throat. He squeezed my heart like a Nerf ball until it was all lumps and fingernail marks. I nursed Pain like a mother. I tried to cheer him up like a sister, but everyone knows how that story goes.

Pain and I did have a few good times, if you can call them that. Eating ice cream under the covers, our tears drying on our cheeks so they chapped. We liked to go to movies alone. Pain, being invisible, snuck in without paying, then he'd leave the seat next to mine and feel up another girl in the theater. I could always tell which one. I'd hear her crying the way I did or crunching her popcorn as though each kernel was a small bone in Pain's neck or foot. He still comes around, though I tell him it's over, though I spit into his round hairy face.

He just laughs that sexy laugh. You know, the kind that gets in your head and you can't tell if it's making you nauseous or turning you on. There's no restraining order that works on Pain, the outlaw who loves to chase and embrace us, the outlaw we sometimes love to chase and embrace.

How Much Is This Poem Going to Cost Me?

It's not something I like to burden my readers with as a rule,
the process of spending money for paper and paper clips, pens,
ink cartridges for the printer—never mind the computer itself
which is a whole other story.
               My favorite uncle
was watching Phil Donahue—the topic was computers I guess—
and a journalist on the panel said, "No writer today
can live without one." My uncle called before the show was over
and offered to buy me my first computer. I dyed my hair red
for the first time, just days before he died. Some readers might think
that might be developed as a separate poem of its own, but since we're all
on tight budgets, I'll try to fit it in here:
               How I called all night
and he wouldn't answer his phone. How my sister found him
early the next morning. The tension over his will.
How my mother picked me up at the train station for the funeral,
crying into my shoulder—her dead older brother

who brought her a hula skirt from the South Pacific after the war,
who gave her away at her wedding since their father
had already passed on—before she suddenly got a grip on herself and said:
"What the hell have you done to your hair?" My mother hates redheads
for some reason, always saying she would have drowned her kids
if any of them had been born strawberry blonde or auburn.
When I was little, my uncle used to live in the apartment downstairs.
That was before his wife died, very young,
so they had never had a chance to have kids. He told me he felt helpless,
it was like watching a dying little bird . . .

                                I pay for this poem in many ways.
Right now, as I write this, I could be at a job earning money
or, at the very least, looking at the help-wanted ads. I could be writing
a screenplay, a novel that would maybe, just maybe, in the end pay for itself.
Sure "there are worse things I could do" as the slutty girl
sings in *Grease*, although it's not politically correct to call her that.
What do people say nowadays? Sexually daring?
I've always liked that character Rizzo—the way she finds out
she's not pregnant after all at the end of the movie,
calling her good news down to her friends
from the highest car on the Ferris wheel.

                                I wish amusement parks
didn't have such high admission prices. And, of course, I still like to eat.
Why just this morning I had a big bowl of cereal. The box says
you can get sixteen servings, but my husband and I never get more than ten,
    which makes
each serving about forty cents, not including the milk
or the banana or the glass of juice. But without that fuel,
who says I could have written this poem? It may have been shorter
and even sadder, because I would have had a hunger headache
and not given it my best.

                    Then there's rent. I can't write this poem outside
as there are no plugs for my computer, and certainly no
surge protectors. I need to be comfortable—a sweat shirt and sweat pants,
which used to be cheaper before everyone started getting into fitness.
I need my glasses more than ever as I get older.
Without insurance, I don't have to tell you how expensive they are.
I need a pair of warm socks and a place to sleep.
Dreams are very important to poets. I need recreation, escape, Hollywood
    movies.
You may remember I made reference to one earlier called *Grease*,

lines 32–38 of this very poem.
                    It's not easy,
now that movies in New York are eight seventy-five.
You get in the theater and smell the buttered popcorn,
though everyone knows it's not really butter they use.
It's more like yellow-colored lard. Any poet with heart trouble
best skip it. But my husband and I smell it
and out come our wallets. The concession stand uses so much salt
every moviegoer also needs a drink, and everyone knows
what those prices are like. We say goodbye to another twenty bucks,
but that's just the beginning—
there are envelopes, bottles of Wite-Out, stamps, and disks.

Thomas Sayers Ellis

Atomic Bride

for Andre Foxxe

A good show
Starts in the
Dressing room

And works its way
To the stage.
Close the door,

Andre's cross-
dressing, what
A drag. All

The world loves
A bride, something
About those gowns.

A good wedding
Starts in the
Department store

And works its way
Into the photo album.
Close the door,

Andre's tying
The knot, what
A drag. Isn't he

Lovely? All
The world loves
A bachelor, some-

thing about glamour
& glitz, white
Shirts, lawsuits.

A good dog
Starts in the yard
And works its way

Into da house.
Close your eyes,
Andre's wide open.

One freak of the week
Per night, what
A drag. Isn't

He lovely? All
The world loves
A nuclear family,

Something about
A suburban home,
Chaos in order.

A good bride starts
In the laboratory
And works his way

To the church.
Close the door,
Andre's thinking

Things over, what
A drag. Isn't
He lovely? All

The world loves
A divorce, something
About broken vows.

A good war starts
In the courtroom
And works its way

To the album cover.
Close the door,
Andre's swearing in,

What a drag.
Isn't he lovely? All
The world loves

A star witness,
Something about
Cross-examination.

A good drug starts
In Washington
And works its way

To the dance floor.
Close the door,
Andre's strung out,

What a drag,
Isn't he lovely? All
The world loves

Rhythm guitar,
Something about
Those warm chords.

A good skeleton
Starts in the closet
And works its way

To the top of the charts.
Start the organ.
Andre's on his way

Down the aisle,
Alone, what an encore. All
The world loves

An explosive ending.
Go ahead Andre
Toss the bouquet.

Star Child

for Garry Shider

Newborn, diaper-clad, same as a child,
That's how you'll leave this world.
No, you won't die, just blast off.

Legs for rockets, bones separating like boosters.
Guitar: a lover, slanted in a hug, plucked,
Scratched, strummed. You will raise

One finger, on the one, for the one,
Then lift like a chorus of neck veins,
All six strings offering redemption.

The black hole at the center
Of the naked universe will respond
With a flash of light: comets, whistles,

Glowing noisemakers, bang, bang.
Roofs everywhere cracking, tearing,
Breaking like water.

Sir Nose D'VoidofFunk

[1]

That name: D'VoidofFunk.
An expressionistic thing

With do-loops
And threes in it,

Preceded by
A silly-serious

Attempt by
Old Smell-O-Vision

To cop
Some nobility.

[2]

The whole bumpnoxious,
Dark thang stanks
Of jivation

And Electric Spank.
Glory, glory, glory—
hallastoopid.

Then there's his funny
Accent—pitch
Change and delay

Looped through
Feedback, pre-spankic
Self-satisfunktion.

Nose gets harder
As his voice
Gets higher.

Nose won't take
His shoes off,
Dance, swim, or sweat,

Nose snores,
A deep snooze,
Snoozation.

[3]

Syndrome tweedle dee dum. Despite
The finger-pointing profile,
False peace signs
And allergic reaction

To light, we brothers
Wanna be down
With Nose. All that!
The girls, the clothes.

Now you know Nose
Knows when to fake it
And when to fake
Faking it.

Waves
Don't mean he's gone
Or that there's going
To be a cover-up,
Very Nixonian.

You can't impeach Nose.
Where's your court-
room, your wig and robe?
You ain't Nose judge.

Somebody scream just to see
The look on our party's
Tromboneless face,
That burial ground

Of samples and clones
Jes grew. A nose
Is a nose is a nose
Is a nose,

      so
Wherever the elephants
In his family
Tree untrunk
Is home.

     [4]

And that's about the only tail
Mugs can push or pin
On him.

Practice

for Derek Walcott

A dank, dark basement entered cautiously from the rear.
     The first thing you saw were bass cabinets,
Their enormous backs an unmovable blackness guarding
The door.
     The first thing you heard was feedback and sometimes
Anthony Ross, our manager's kid brother, snare-
And pedal-less, pretending to kick.
     The floor was worried with slithering cords,
Living wires that lifted and looped like vines of verse.
     The cold brick walls were covered with noise
And, like it or not, several mouth-orange cardboard posters
—those trifling, Day-Glo ones that resembled sores
When the lights were on, and sores
When they were off.
     The air was thick with Chinese take-out, reverb,
The young girls on us, and designer cologne.
     An orphaned microphone slept on a pillow at the bottom
Of the bass drum's navel-less, belly-impersonating, soul-shaped O

—its sense of responsibility made more evenly percussive by
A pair of congas repeatedly nursing their newborn bongos,
All meter and rhythm at once; neither dissing the pocket.

   Floor tom. Two-faced cymbals. A hint of high-hat.
Sticks.

   Our drummer sat facing all of this, caged, while our entire
Frontline (female vocalist included) worked out,
Breathing and counting and stepping
Like odd numbers.

   Big Earl and Scarecrow stood behind guitars the same way
The marines at The Tomb of the Unknown Soldier
Stood behind rifles.

   The timbales and rototoms side-by-side were
Like a finish line of chrome, the bridge (each
And every other groove) a horn's valved prose
Asked for, asked for, asked for.

Suzanne Gardinier

Democracy

Nothing hurts but the foot is insistent
The foot seeps The foot has never healed
The foot pierced and swollen will not be hidden
The foot will at all costs be included
The foot will unburden The foot will rule
waking and sleep until it's attended
Attention The foot has something to say
but no way of speaking The foot is sealed
and drums the ground in coded unvocable
syllables The foot has a story
the foot can't tell The foot draws near
to weeping to the silver abundance
of stacked fish to fire to amputations
to the trading of copper cocoa and tin
to the spraying of passersby with rounds
of ammunition to the transfer of deeds
to the spewing of muttered words from the tried
and vanished to notices of eviction
to braids of rawhide with salt-stiff handles
to turkey and cranberry suppers to
the holds of ships to forcings on rooftops
and on pine needles to quahogs and muskets
to blocks of auction and execution
The foot pats the dirt garbled growing
tired but not resting The foot continues

Admirals (Columbus)

The people go naked men and women
of handsome bodies and very good faces
On the first Island I took some by force

that they might give information They remained
so much our friends that it was a marvel
Thus the eternal God our Lord gives
victory to those who follow His way
They swam to the ships and brought us water
They are so free with all they possess
none would believe without having seen it
Of anything they have they give
with as much love as if they gave their hearts
Of keen intelligence they navigate
all these seas but are timid beyond cure
They bear no arms nor know thereof
When I showed them swords they grasped by the blade
and cut themselves in ignorance They have
no iron Their spears are made of cane
It seems they belong to no religion
They are of the opinion that I and my ships
come from the source of all power and goodness
the sky In all the world there are no
better people no better country
With fifty men we could subjugate them
and make them do whatever we want

The Ghost of Santo Domingo

I've set six stones in a row near the eastern
shore above where the tide can touch them
to mark the time gone since they took her away
My feet trace the usual paths past cooksmoke
the place where she slept But inside something
has changed I dream the night of her first blood
celebrated in the circle of women
dancing singing silence Then there is
rope and her nails and screaming pushed into
sand her perfect integrity torn
to scraps scattered over the waves Her body
becomes the body of our village then
of the island then of all the land and sea

and sky we know and the hunters of souls
shake the stains of the bloody division
from their beards and clothes They drive hands from wrists
They split tongues and bury them but still
they tell and tell I saw everything My daughter
is no longer what I was taught to call
alive Neither am I permitted
to lay her with her people join the broken
circle I have each morning's watching
over the water where she disappeared
and these six stones set in a line whose ends
run from each other and refuse to meet

Two Girls

> who come in the night whispering

Whose songs are too small to remember
Whose rest Whose gestures disappeared
To look for them without a sentence
To make a shelter for them here
One night dancer One firstlight singer
Who mark each lost nearness with tears
One torn cloth coat One pact unmended
Who warn in whispers fifty years
One who wants the word for morning
Two we think are here no longer
One who wants the word for footprint
Two girls tangled in the branches
One in smoke One in shadow
One from bridges One from snow
> *Kaddish*
The languages of wrists and ankles
Winter Soup Bread A woman's neck
Sealed train to suddenly an island
Here she who lay down her small flesh
This crow This star This metal bramble
This path where craft and bodies mesh
This night chimney This ditch This shamble

To manufacture smoke from breath
What you know of masks Of making
Forest clearing built of ashes
Nachtwache The word for footprint
All the songs you have forgotten
This ghost fury This disguise
Borrowed mouth and borrowed eyes
at exactly 8:15 a.m. a thousand doves released from cages
Mountain flanks Barley Delta bridges
Salt river's movement in the heat
Summer Daughter Breakfast Two fishes
Shadows The language shadows speak
A cricket Just before the brightness
She who watches She who has seen
Invention heralded by engines
This labor's fruit This planned machine
Straw umbrellas Coats of paper
Temples choked with unclaimed ashes
Thirst *Zenshō* The word for morning
She who could not keep her skin on
You who call her No Witness
You who think she found her rest
You
Her hair smoothed back from fever forehead
Her chill in nearness put away
The fledgling kept The sapling guarded
These two who knock with every rain
Where there is warmth Where there is water
The stamping songs of yesterday
Two guardians Two raging daughters
You who were taught another way
You who think a word is useless
You who mock and doubt your dreaming
You who know dirt is not holy
You who never were a child
Archipelago Cistern
You hungry You thirsty Turn

Nachtwache: night watchman
Zenshō: conflagration

Letter to My Mother

"Goodbye" is not quite true; we'll meet tonight
as we do at night, in various disguises
through acres of dreams, though in another country
you cook alone and riffle through the bills.
When I tongue the envelope to seal it
I see the two of us, the year we slept
together, my mouth rose around your breast.
These thin sheets I write on aren't so different
from those that covered us: insubstantial,
vulnerable to wind, to sudden tearing.

Each woman keeps a secret: that her first love
was a woman, even if she later turned
to others. Now the pleasure of a bowl
of cherries, still warm from the tree, is never
far from danger; if I burst the fruit against
my teeth, recklessly, over and over,
your body may rise up, first food, first pleasure,
naming all the other imitations,
claiming me, sealing my mouth over
with yours, the kiss I dream about and dread.

I made my mind up early on that you
would be more independent than I was —
instead you gave the package you'd been given:
bottles, useless matches, chips of sobs,
all broken, like a lamp sent through the mail.
Here where I am the box holds only letters.
But even here, where the language I must speak
is not the one I learned from you, the landscape
daily touches deeper, olives bend
over the mountain, cypress grips the steep

embankment, and the more I look I love.
Every helpless time your voice is with me,
your skin, your smells, the beating of your heart.
I can't help thinking you would be more happy
if you could forget—your anger, pounded
flat, like foil hung among the cherries
to scare the birds, has beauty of its own.
When the south wind strips leaves from the plane trees
every gust is your unspoken wanting:
hot, strong, pitilessly dry.

I want hills blanked in snow, all sound muffled,
still and cold, colorless, to soothe
the upsurge of angry love and sadness
your letter brings. Everywhere I go
since first leaving you I am the lover
who celebrates and heals. You taught me. Now
you're my only failure: hunched with morning
coffee, or at night hollowed by work,
then hammered into sleep. My exiled power
comes to nothing: the bite of postmarks, ink.

James Harms

My Androgynous Years

I had a crisis at the supermarket, yesterday.
I said to myself softly, so no one could hear,
I said, Your soul is *not* stepping
from your body. I said, Stop it, relax.
And I did. I held it all together
past the magazines and gum,
through 8-Items-or-Less and out the door.
I sat in my car and let mascara
run down my arms like greasy rain.
Until a woman in a Volvo beeped
and pointed at the asphalt under me,
unwilling, I guess, to wait any longer.
When I was eight my sister hated me.
She hated clothes and make-up.
She hated buckled shoes.
We'd walk Vermilion Street beneath
the insect sizzle of neon
to buy my mother cigarettes,
loiter like felons till
all seemed clear in Lee's Liquor-Mart.
I'd ask Peter Lee where the Cokes had gone,
and he'd come around to help me look
while my sister snaked her hand to a packet
of Pall Malls and was gone. On the way home,
sometimes, she ran ahead, easy over long legs.
She'd find a crumbling vestibule
to soothe her shadow down to stone
and time my slow arrival.
We'd sit near a puddle of ragwater
or piss, her laughter a hand against
my neck, and wait for my sobs to soften.
I share my lunch today with a boy from
Peru, Indiana. He recites King's
"I Have a Dream" speech,.

rising off the bench to shake his fists
at the assembled phantoms.
Pigeons scatter and regather, and all around us
haloes appear and vanish, the fountain mist
blown in rainbows and to pieces.
He is splendid and I offer all my Fritos.
One night he will come to me like a dream
on the television and announce
a special offer: laser-sharpened knives
or a three-record set.
But that's the future. For now
we hold hands and talk about the news,
which is much better than yesterday's
but only half as good as tomorrow's.

The Joy Addict

Whales fall slowly to the ocean floor
after dying and feed the vertical nation
for years. Like Christ, who feeds us still,
they say, though I don't know.
But imagine it:
fish chasing through the bones
or nibbling what's left, the whale,
when it finally touches bottom,
an empty church.
Forget all that,
it's intended to soften
the skin, like apricot seeds and mud, or boredom.
The drift of worlds in a given day
can turn a telephone to porcelain,
open graves in the sidewalk. So that
who knows why thinking about thinking
leads to new inventions of grace
that never take, never lead to, say, what to do
with Grandmother, who is determined to live
"beyond her usefulness," which is fine,
but why won't she relax and watch the sea with me?

I wish someone would intrude on all this.
People grow tired
explaining themselves to mirrors,
to clerks administering the awful perfume.
I ask a Liberace look-alike,
"Why do you dress that way?"
"What way?" he says,
and he's right.
Who taught us to bow our heads
while waiting for trains? to touch
lumber without regret and sing privately
or not at all? to invest the season
with forgiveness and coax from it
a hopeful omen? Lord knows
the hope would heal this little fear.
But who taught us to fear?
Soon branches crackle in the windy heat
like something cooking too quickly,
dogwood lathering the empty woods
and everyone looking for a commitment
of permanence, from summer, from someone else.
Two deer the color of corn disappear
into an empty field, and I wait beside the road
for them to move. I want to see them again.

Los Angeles, the Angels

Doves love a dying palm. They nestle in the loud fronds. They hum
and shiver. The way days end here: no click; no door sealing in the light.
The way dusk enters the room and embitters it; the way
the paint absorbs its shadows, the skin absorbing stares.

I hear you and I hate it. I hate hearing your voice in the leaves
as I sand down the bureau; I drag out the furniture, drag it out
onto the driveway but still, *How have you come so far
without belief?* I rake the yard to muffle your voice.

Evening is slithering toward me, and behind it, believe me,
the cold. Night is a chance to see the stars as they were
when Greeks in their shifts and leather slippers, their
gruesome beards sandy and caked with salt—before turning
toward each other in sleep—listened, terrified, to the laughter
breaking with the waves, the slim sheet of water drawing close.

And their dreams were worn as singlets in the next day's race,
the cloth of sleep sewn into waking, the long day of sleep.
Because they knew, as I have chosen not to—each turn at the wheel
a chance to drive my purchases and children to a clear spot
on the hillside—they knew what we would become: old thieves
in beaten-up cars, idling at the signals, skin going bad in the sun.

Night is a wind blowing away the light, which streaks and burns
on its way west. Night is an empty lung and here's the moon:
the armoire mounts a broken dresser; the lawn grows plastic chairs.
How can I forgive you? How have you come so far? I rake
the dark shards from the grass, your voice in pieces, *so far, belief.*

Soon

He had always supposed he would die first,
before her, though he didn't think about it much.
It was like a secret learned and then forgotten,
a letter that hurts and is hidden away in a trunk.
But he had always assumed that one of many gifts
she would give him would be to bury him,
and that was that, though now and then,
as he cleaned her hair from the drain or
sliced an apple into wedges for lunch, placing
half on a yellow plate for her, eating the rest
as he stood reading her shopping list taped
to the refrigerator, now and then he thought
of how much harder it is to be left behind,
and for a while he'd feel an ache in his hands,
as if he were trying to hold onto something
too tightly. Twenty-five years ago she was already

twenty years younger than he, sitting outside
his office, her name on a sheet of paper tacked
to the door, her name with others, each listed
by the hour: it was always three o'clock with her,
always Wednesdays. And he loved her immediately,
though of course, he hadn't known it right away.
Perhaps one day, as she pulled her books from a bag
and began to ask a question, pointing at a line in a poem,
perhaps he thought of how much harder it would be for her,
perhaps he thought this before he'd ever kissed her,
before he noticed how her glance left a streak
on his cheek for days, as if her thoughts could touch,
could leave the small bruises love leaves early on.
But even then there was nothing he could do about it.
Once, years after, he awoke from a dream where
he had watched her from a stand of black oaks
as she dropped a daisy in his grave. And later,
still dreaming, he had circled in the air above their bed
as she tossed loosely in the sheets without him,
like an empty cup blown with paper down the street;
she had been wearing a shirt he'd left dirty in the hamper.
She wrapped her arms around his pillow
as though it were a sack of stones, as though it held her
in place on the earth, kept her from rising to join him.
And when he drifted on her breath out the open window,
he had reached to grab the curtains; he had wanted
to stay with her, though he was nothing then, a breeze,
his hands passing through the thin fabric like smoke
through a screen. And for the rest of the dream
he wandered through their town disrupting
leaves gathered in the gutters, cooling a hot cheek here
and there: a breeze. He never told her of his dream.
Sometimes he watched her from the porch as she stooped
and straightened in the small side garden.
He watched her pull the carrots from the earth,
how she shook them gently before dropping them
in the basket. She wore around her neck
a small woven sack on a string and in it kept
a quarter: if ever far from home and stranded
she could call. But she was never far from home.
And the sack lifted away from her breast as she bent

to pull a weed; it swung back and forth
like a hypnotist's watch; she took it off only
to sleep. And when he awoke before her each morning
he thought of her alone in the empty house
tending to the three cats, winding the clocks,
the few things he now did, stacking logs
on the front porch each October, phoning for oil
when the furnace went cold, filling the feeder
by the kitchen door. And of course it hurt him
to imagine her alone, as it hurts him now
to imagine what becomes of those who go, or worse,
of those who stay behind as wind, as small eddies of air.
He gathers the laundry in piles, wonders where
she kept the bleach. He lifts the sash, lets in
a soft wind hoping for the smell of lilacs,
though it's early yet, only April. He will have to wait
for lilacs and for whatever she planted in the garden.
It is too soon to know for sure what is there.

Allison Joseph

Numbers

My father taught me to measure
the worth of any good thing
by the number of black people
involved. Without sufficient numbers,

he wouldn't root for a team,
wouldn't eat in a restaurant,
wouldn't turn on his television
to watch the local newscast

that didn't have a black anchor.
He wanted black people
to appear on *Masterpiece Theatre*
—he'd lived in England so he knew

black people lived there—
wanted us on *Evening at Pops*
and *Live from Wolf Trap*,
the orchestra's black musicians

conveniently placed up front
for his recognition, wanted
every diva who performed at the Met
to be brown, proud, beautiful—

an endless string of Jessye Normans
and Leontyne Prices. He'd rage
at commercials, at *The Brady Bunch*,
at soap operas, Broadway musicals,

at any bit of American culture
tossed before us as entertainment
that dared not have a black cast member.
So I grew up rooting against the then

all-white Mets, the Boston Red Sox
(Jim Rice their only saving grace),
the Celtics, hell, the whole city of Boston,
the obscene snowy landscape of New England.

So he probably thought he'd failed
to instill the wisest lesson
when we drove to that college
in middle-of-nowhere Ohio

with its green clapboard shutters
on its white colonial cottages,
its manicured hedges
and windowboxes of tulips.

Resolute, he helped me hoist boxes
to my narrow, undecorated room,
watched glumly as Mom unpacked
suitcases, as my sister folded clothes.

Suspicious, he finally asked,
where are all the black people,
but I could show him only three faces
in the freshman picture book,

including my own photo-booth snapshot.
He thought I was crazy to live
so close to them, the white people
who'd conspired so long against him,

the numbers on that campus
far too low for him, my scholarship
bleaching me, making me
less black, less daughter.

Pure Pop

for Matthew Sweet

Why is it that women
can fall for any man

talented enough to get his face
on an album cover, no matter

how handsome or how worn
that face happens to be?

Face it, girls, we've
swooned over some pretty

strange specimens—Sinatra
and Bing in their beanpole

crooner days, Buddy Holly
in his bottle-thick glasses

stuttering declarations
of love, bigger-than-life

Barry White seducing us with
violin swells, serious bass.

Maybe that's why
I find myself listening

to Matthew's lovesick songs again,
his voice quavering on the ballads,

bold when the music's uptempo,
so catchy I can't stop singing

along, though I know
it's silly for me to mimic him,

as if I want the woman he wants,
both of us going unfulfilled.

What I really want is him,
hair spilling over one eye,

his guitar talk late at night,
his uncertain smile that can't

explain why his songs always buzz
in my head. I thought I could shake this,

that I'd soon grow tired of listening
to a man who sounds more like

a boy wonder, that I'd find
better pleasures than this pure pop,

a guy with a guitar who frets
far too much over breaking up, making up.

Matthew, if you're listening,
don't get a whiz-kid agent

who'll slick your hair back,
don't trade your guitar

for a glitzy synthesizer,
don't tan in hopes of a

Las Vegas career, and don't you
dare lift weights at some mirrored

health club. I want you to stay
just as you are in this photo—

morose, pale, never satisfied
with love's changes, enduring them anyway

for the right girl
at the right moment.

My Father's Heroes

Not JFK, not MLK,
certainly not Ronald Reagan
or Edward I. Koch,
no, instead my father
chose to glory in the feats
of Cool Papa Bell, quickest
man in the Negro Leagues,
able, Dad bragged,
to flick off a light switch,
then dart into bed
before the room went dark.
Praising the fast-dancing feet
of the Nicolas brothers,
he called my attention to
their rapid-fire acrobatics
but saved his true love
for Peg Leg Bates,
the one-legged tap dancer
who'd pound out a furious rhythm
on his wooden leg,
dazzling audiences
with leaps, hops, bounds.
I never saw Father
anywhere near a piano,
but he still schooled me
about Jimmy Rushing—
"Mister Five by Five,"
tagged so because
he stood five feet tall
and looked five feet wide,
had me humming Jelly Roll Morton's
creole jazz though he'd never
been near New Orleans,
made certain I knew the difference
between Fats Domino and Fats Waller,
played me the Harlem rhapsodies
of Ellington so loudly I thought
the orchestra had come to visit,
Sir Duke himself in our living

room, elegant in top hat, tails.
To Dad, Satchmo and Satchel Paige
both deserved equal praise;
equal adulation was given
to the theatrics of Louie Jordan
as he belted out rhythm and blues tunes
about hard-headed women like "Caldonia,"
the hi-de-ho of Cab Calloway
as he spun tales of "Minnie the Moocher,"
regal in yards of zoot suit,
and to the sublime grace of "Mr. B.",
Billy Eckstine crooning smoother
than any white man.
Coleman Hawkins, Lester Young,
Bird and Diz all came to play
from our raspy console hi-fi,
its needle worn, jumping over scratches.

But some mornings,
I'd wake to hear a woman's voice
filling our rooms with trembling
love songs, a voice so vulnerable
even I understood, even though
the language was French,
the singer white, female.
This, he'd say, is Piaf,
the little sparrow,
and I'd listen to that voice
send it's sorrows through our house
and I knew that what touched my father
wasn't always race, wasn't always color.
Somehow he knew I needed
to hear this woman sing
from her fragile bones,
her sound silencing us both,
as her crowds in Paris must have been
when they saw her tiny figure
on the stage, bent over to sing
the last vestiges of a ballad,
the last words
she'd give them.

Julia Kasdorf

When Our Women Go Crazy

When our women go crazy, they're scared there won't be
enough meat in the house. They keep asking
but how will we eat? Who will cook? Will there be enough?
Mother to daughter, it's always the same
questions. The sisters and aunts recognize symptoms:
       she thinks there's no food, same as Mommy
       before they sent her away to that place,
       and she thinks if she goes, the men will eat
       whatever they find right out of the saucepans.
When our women are sane, they can tomatoes
and simmer big pots of soup for the freezer.
They are satisfied arranging spice tins
on cupboard shelves lined with clean paper.
They save all the leftovers under tight lids
and only throw them away when they're rotten.
Their refrigerators are always immaculate and full,
which is also the case when our women are crazy.

Grossdaadi's Funeral

This is the child in a buff-colored coat with a foxtail collar.
This is the child who walks down the aisle between straight-back benches
in Amish church; gapes at great aunts and great uncles and covens of cousins in
    black.

This is the child whose momma knows she'll see plenty of this
and lifts her to the bare, pine box that Grossdaadi made for himself.
(He crawled in to test, then kept it locked in a spare bedroom back at the farm.)

This is the child who stares at his hand, bony and veined,
covered with skin like the paper her momma wraps sandwiches in;
she touches his face chilled by the aunts who sat up all night
sponging the corpse.

This is the child who fingers his beard, as gray as the fur
on the foxhead muff that dangles from grosgrain around her neck.
Later she'll learn the hair of the dead—like this dirty gauze beard—
still grows in the grave.

This is the girl who clutches the muff, who digs in its fur
for edges of skull, scrapes at the glass beads glued in for eyes,
and presses the teeth so her fingertips sting
all through the long, German prayers.

Mennonites

We keep our quilts in closets and do not dance.
We hoe thistles along fence rows for fear
we may not be perfect as our Heavenly Father.
We clean up his disasters. No one has to
call; we just show up in the wake of tornadoes
with hammers, after floods with buckets.
Like Jesus, the servant, we wash each other's feet
twice a year and eat the Lord's Supper,
afraid of sins hidden so deep in our organs
they could damn us unawares,
swallowing this bread, his body, this juice.
Growing up, we love the engravings in *Martyr's Mirror:*
men drowned like cats in burlap sacks,
the Catholic inquisitors,
the woman who handed a pear to her son,
her tongue screwed to the roof of her mouth
to keep her from singing hymns while she burned.
We love Catherine the Great and the rich tracts
she gave us in the Ukraine, bright green winter wheat,
the Cossacks who torched it, and Stalin,
who starved our cousins while wheat rotted

in granaries. We must love our enemies.
We must forgive as our sins are forgiven,
our great-uncle tells us, showing the chain
and ball in a cage whittled from one block of wood
while he was in prison for refusing to shoulder
a gun. He shows the clipping from 1916:
Mennonites are German milksops, too yellow to fight.
We love those Nazi soldiers who, like Moses,
led the last cattle cars rocking out of the Ukraine,
crammed with our parents—children then—
learning the names of Kansas, Saskatchewan, Paraguay.
This is why we cannot leave the beliefs
or what else would we be? Why we eat
'til we're drunk on shoofly and moon pies and borscht.
We do not drink; we sing. Unaccompanied on Sundays,
those hymns in four parts, our voices lift with such force
that we lift, as chaff lifts toward God.

Green Market, New York

The first day of false spring, I hit the street
buoyant, my coat open. I could keep walking
and leave that job without cleaning my desk.
At Union Square, the country people slouch
by crates of last fall's potatoes.
An Amish lady tends her table of pies.
I ask her where her farm is. "Upstate," she says,
"but we moved from P.A. where the land is better
and the growing season's longer by a month."
I ask where in P.A. "Towns you wouldn't know,
around Mifflinburg, around Belleville."
And I tell her I was born there.
"Now who would your grandparents be?"
"Thomas and Vesta Peachey."
"Well, I was a Peachey," she says,
and she grins like she sees the whole farm
on my face. "What a place your folks had,
down Locust Grove. Do you know my father,

the harness shop on the Front Mountain Road?"
I do. And then we can't think of what to say,
that Valley so far from the traffic on Broadway.
I choose a pie while she eyes my short hair
then looks square on my face. She knows
I know better than to pay six dollars for this.
"Do you live in the city?" she asks, "do you like it?"
I say no. And that was no lie, Emma Peachey.
I don't like New York, but sometimes these streets
hold me as hard as we're held by rich earth.
I have not forgotten that Bible verse:
Whoever puts his hand to the plow and looks back
is not fit for the Kingdom of God.

Eve's Striptease

Lingerie shopping with Mom, I braced myself
for the wedding night advice. Would I seem
curious enough, sufficiently afraid? Yet
when we sat together on their bed, her words
were surprisingly wise:
           Whatever else happens, remember this—
           it keeps getting better and better.
She had to be telling the truth. At ten,
I found a jar of Vaseline in her nightstand,
its creamy grease gouged deep, and dusting
their room each week, I marked the decline
of bedside candles. But she didn't say lust
is a bird of prey or tell me the passion
she passed on to me is no protector of borders.
She'd warned me only about the urges men get
and how to save myself from them. Though
she'd flirt with any greenhouse man
for the best cabbage flats, any grease monkey
under the hood, she never kissed anyone but Dad.
How could she guess that with *Jesus Loves Me*
on my tongue, constantly suffering crushes
on uncles, I would come to find that

almost everything gets better and better?
The tiny bird she set loving in me must
keep on, batting the bars of its cage
in a rage only matched by my cravings
for an ample pantry and golden anniversary.
She let me learn for myself all the desires
a body can hold, how they grow stronger
and wilder with age, tugging in every direction
until it feels my sternum might split
like Adam's when Eve stepped out,
sloughing off ribs.

Joy Katz

Women Must Put Off Their Rich Apparel

Women must put off their rich apparel;
at midday they must disrobe.

Apart from men are the folds of sleep,
daylight's frank remarks: the skin

of the eye, softening, softening.
Women must put on plainness,

the sweet set of the mouth's line;
the body must surface, the light,

the muscled indifference of deer.
A woman must let love recede,

the carved-out ribs sleep,
the vessel marked in bird lines

empty, as the sea empties her.
Say the sea, sound of leaves, the old

devotion, the call and response.
Reeds, caves, shoulders of cypress,

the woman who at this moment
does not need the world.

Concerning the Islands Newly Discovered

And there we spent the night, where they offered us
their women, and we were unable to fend them off.
—Amerigo Vespucci

Your Magnificent Lord,
having known the continual struggle
man undergoes in
praiseworthy new lands . . .

The good harbor, amaranth, trees like our willows
which drag the curve of cove like women's hair
falling

—The women especially,

                    their long black hair
          which makes them beautiful

It matters little to them if their appetite comes at midnight

The women are of noble body and we gave them
some of our things such as bells,
mirrors, glass beads

We took from them many things
                    more praiseworthy and enduring

though of little value

Well may Your Magnificence forgive me
if I desire to remain—

if, nightly
alone in the ship's hold
I dig my hands into barrels of bells, glass beads,
mirrors, as if I am swimming . . .

Taxonomy

Language is only an instrument for the attainment of science
Jefferson wrote Marbois
among the columns of names—
Senna, snake-root, lupine, Cherokee plum
At Poplar Forest, he planted rows of scaly bark hickory,
measured fisted buds of poke.

*

Random stokes and knots, scribbles
of hair on the crushed, sweat-drenched linen
of his wife's pillow as she lay dying.
Present occupations disable me from completing
the Notes, he wrote. His fingers brushed
dovetailed corners of coffin—
his infant daughter's. Outside,
jasmine and wethawk in the marbled cold
of spring sky.
                    Royston crow, towhee,
and the sting of Tarleton in the wide, shallow mouths
of common salt near Monticello.

*

Nights he walked ragged, trampled rows
of cabbage to the line of small shacks, yellow oil
lamplight, a neighborhood of slaves.
The spirit of the master is abating.

*

You can stand on a cliff before the heave and tear
in Jefferson's mountains, in the sublime,
and not escape the awe. You can kneel above the abyss,
two hundred and seventy feet
of gouged rock and silver threads of stream, your back
to silver grilles of cars parked row on row in searing sun.
Here the eye ultimately composes itself
Jefferson added later, much later—looking away to the plain,
away from the arch that sprung

as it were, up to heaven.

The Imperfect Is Our Paradise

An orange leaf on every finger bowl: a dozen tongues
mute about their clear water and their own orange scent

and the way the glass pressures the heavy, white-flossed linen
a little, as a cat flattens grass in the yard.

Suppose that this complete simplicity
is the torment itself, delighting nothing of the vital I?

The wainscoting smiles in refraction through the clear water;
the horned cone of the whelk catches the frank daylight

from the window, and so appears whiter than the white freesia
in its vase. I don't know how to live with beauty.

Even the held breath of expectation enlarges it—
places set for guests to sing and slap the table

until the silver jumps like fish from their boisterous grace.
When the walls were wet I loved that particular blue.

The height of the flowers through the door's arch
is another thing I can't escape. The trouble is the stillness,

the *not* desiring so much more than this: an orange leaf
on every finger bowl.

Falling

1. Proserpina

She got pulled down and learned to like it. It happened gradually, from the
warmth maybe, the moans . . . all those half-years in hell and one day a murmur,
almost somnolent, *all right then, fuck me in the ass.*

This was the day she returned, bloodied and dreamy, one broken heel and dress inside out, to the frozen earth—the first time spring came late. Ceres knew then she had lost her. Blanched almonds and fennel, boiled wheat, white seeds, offerings for the dead; Ceres bit her fingerpads until they burst like grapes.

2. Heroin

What would happen, they said, is that we would like it, and then we would do anything for it. The drug seemed like chalk dust or powdered orchids, and I dreamed at night about the needle:

dragonfly metal and a barrel like clouds, plunger pushing waves of liquid like melted nacre. It would feel like clouds, I imagined—"opiate," opaline slipping-down feeling of sleep coming on. They would push the tine into the nearly-finned skin between my toes, the tiny veins—

I ran into my mother's bed, clenched my legs to my chest, clenched my feet into my hands, and lay awake all night sweating and cleaving. I would like it. I would like it like heaven and would be lost.

Timothy Liu

Ariel Singing

It is not happiness. Not the man standing
in line waiting to show me his poppies
and doves. Not a vase or an empty cage
he leaves when the magic act is over.
It is sleeping for a long time, the rest
of the world standing in a broken line.
Or waking without new flowers flaming
into this world. It is a world without song
I flew right into. In the glass I saw
one soul, not two colliding into one.
Nothing shattered. What is fragile came after,
time to kill. We love badly. Do you see
how we lie awake, always hungry in bed?
The priests continue to hold out their fast
offerings to the weak. Amen. Teach me
how to sing in a grove of olive trees,
to fall as a sparrow. It is all I want.

Vox Angelica

I sing to a breeze that runs through the rafters.
A woman skins a snake. She turns
but not enough for me to see her face.
In the sink, the peelings have begun to pile up
in a mound the color of dirt.
She hears the oil hissing on its own
and thinks of throwing something in—
ginger, garlic, chopped rings of green onion—
but doesn't, lets the oil brown
until the smoke rises
and fills the dark corners of the kitchen.

The birds tonight are louder than ever,
perched beside a river of flying fish.

                            *

The sweat on her feverish face
dissipates, flying upward
to God as she clings to the shoulders
of death, her feet touching
neither heaven nor earth.
They say death has a nobility of its own
but all she could hear was weeping—
not entirely a human sound
but a sound as if made by a machine
that played again and again
like a tape she could not erase.
She tried to explain the sadness,
the leaves changing to a color
she could no longer describe.

                            *

The hour of the Bible is dead.
Neither dirt nor flowers
can keep her body warm enough.
Driving from the service,
I keep my hands on the wheel
as if steadying myself
the way silence holds each word in place.
I imagine lying down next to her
as earth is sprinkled over our eyes,
our mouths filling with dirt.

                            *

The angels are singing
in the shadows of the house,
night a black cat sitting on my chest,
claws extended toward my face,
the scar on my body
a witness to that place where the world
had once been opened, muscle
and blood. How a vision
pinned me down until my scream

reached two worlds
on both sides of the glass.
Everything happened twice
in the cat's eyes,
the slow engine of happiness
seducing me back to sleep.

*

The words I speak I cannot revise.
All art is an afterthought,
an attempt to interpret a dream
that by its nature is perfected,
the bed unmade, and me almost late
to my next appointment where more of me
must get cut out. The horror
of getting beyond the skin,
the small white aberration that I dreamed
would not grow back, not enlarge
to fill my entire conscious body.
I think of how the mystics read
by the light of their own bodies.
What a world of darkness that must have been
to read by the flaming hearts
that turn into heaps of ash on the altar,
how everything in the end is made
equal by the wind.

Kindertotenlieder

Another fire dying down, the view from here
about to change—my father listening to Mahler
late into the afternoon, a scripture torn

from the family Bible floating upward on a bed
of its own ashes, unable to withstand

a child's magnifying glass. (As if a girl
could just lie down in the middle of the road
while her bicycle continued on without her . . .)

My father dreaming of a better world where girls
don't suddenly turn into a boat of flowers—

diamonds of safety glass strewn on a gravel road
where old men wander into the night to rest
their heads on bales of hay, the countryside full

of barns braced against the wind. (Tell us where
the rain has gone.) A woman closes her mouth

for forty years, and we say the world is a place
charred by the sun, no moon or stars in a barn
where that truck raised high on concrete blocks

waits for a pane of tinted glass—a childhood
we almost had through which to view the world.

Poem

Late butterflies gliding through the air—

how else to begin without a mouth
full of pins? Life is more

than chrysalis. There are voices

in the earth, a vengeance you can taste
in all our crops. The monarchs

are dying out, some say whole streams

gone to rust that once meandered down
to Mexico. Our resident toad

returns no more. Only children

on the sidewalk writing stories in chalk
under blue pines dusted with wings

that flutter out of their lives.

Sunday

And when they sat down in the morning
to bowls of cold cereal, each in turn
would notice the blades of a ceiling fan
spinning at the bottom of their spoons,
small enough to swallow, yet no one
ever mentioned it, neither looking up
nor into each other's eyes for fear
of feeding the hunger that held them there.

Khaled Mattawa

Heartsong

A bird sings from the tree. The bird sings
sending waves of desire—and I stand on my roof
waiting for a randomness to storm my days. I stand on my roof
filled with the longing that sings its way out of the bird.
And I am afraid that my call will break me,
the cry blocked by my tongue will pronounce me mad.
O bird mad with longing, O balancing bar,
tightrope, monkey grunting from a roof. Fortunate bird.
I stand on my roof and wave centuries of desire.
I am the Bedouin pondering the abandoned campsite
licking the ashes of the night fire; the American walking
walking miles of dresses, blouses, and skirts
filling them with infinite lovers;
the mystic feeling the pull swirling in his chest,
a desert of purpose expanding and burning and yellowing
every shade of green. And I stand on my roof.
And I say come like a stranger, like a feather
falling on an old woman's shoulder, like a hawk
that comes to feed from her hands, come like a mystery,
like sunlight rain, a blessing, a bus falling off a bridge,
come like a deserting soldier, a murderer chased by law,
like a girl prostitute escaping her pimp, come like a lost horse,
like the last day on earth, come like a sigh from a sick man,
come like a whisper, like a bump on the road, like a flood,
a dam breaking, turbines falling from the sky,
come love like the stench of a swamp, a barrage of light
filling a blind girl's eye, come like a memory
convulsing the body into sobs, like a carcass floating on a stream,
come like a vision, come love like a crushing need,
come like an afterthought. Heart song. Heart song.
The pole smashes and the live wires yellow streaks
on the lush grass. Come look and let me wonder.
Someone. So many. The sounds of footsteps, horses, and cars.
Come look and let me wonder. And I stand on my roof

echoing the bird's song, and the world says: Do not sleep.
Do not sleep now that you have housed your longing
within the pain of words.

Watermelon Tales

January. Snow. For days I have craved
          watermelons, wanted
    to freckle the ground with seeds,
to perform a ritual:
         Noontime, an early
    summer Sunday, the village
chief faces north, spits seven mouthfuls,
        fingers a circle
    around a galaxy of seeds.

            *

Maimoon the Bedouin visited in
        summer, always with
    a gift: a pickup truck load
of watermelons. "Something for
        the children," he explained.
    Neighbors brought wheelbarrows to
fetch their share. Our chickens ate the rest.

            *

       His right ear pricked up
    close, my father taps on a
watermelon, strokes as though it were
        a thigh. A light slap.
    "If it doesn't sound like your hands
clapping at a wedding, it's not yours."

            *

Men shake their chief's hand,
children kiss it. Everyone files
behind him when he walks back. No one
talks until the tomb
of the local saint. The rich
place coin sacks at his feet, the poor leave
cups of melon seeds.

*

Maimoon also brought us meat,
gazelles he rammed with his truck.
His daughter, Selima,
said he once swerved off the road
suddenly, drove for an hour until
he spotted six. He hadn't
hit any when the truck ran out
of gas. Thirty yards away the gazelles
stood panting, and he
ran to catch one with his bare hands.

*

Two choices, my father's doctor tell us:
transplant or six months
of pain. Outside his office,
I point to a fruit stall, the seller
waving off flies with
a feather fan. My father
strokes, slaps, and when I lift the melon
to my shoulder says
"Eleven years in America
and you carry a watermelon
like a peasant!"

*

Uncle Abdellah buries
a watermelon underneath the
   approach of the waves—
"Like a refrigerator
down there." It's July, a picnic at
   Tokara Beach. We're
  kicking a ball when
my brother trips hard on the hole. He's
   told to eat what he'd
  broken too soon. I watched him
swallow pulp, seed, salt, and sand.

       *

  Her shadow twice her
  height, the village sorceress
walks to where the chief spat. She reveals
   size of the harvest,
  chance of drought, whose sons will wed
whose daughters, and names of elders whose
   ailments will not cease.

       *

  Selima told the gazelle
story sitting in a tub. With soap,
  my mother scrubbed the girl's scalp,
tossing handfuls of foam against
   the white tile. She then
  poured kerosene on Selima's
hair, rubbed till lice slid down her face,
   combed till the tines
  filled with the dead.

       *

Selima married. My mother sent her
          a silver anklet,
     a green silk shawl, and decided
against an ivory comb. My father paid
          the sheikh to perform
     the wedding. A week later
at his door, the sheikh found three water-
          melons and a gazelle-
     skin prayer rug, a tire mark
across the spot where he would have rested his
          head in prostration.

                    *

     I cut the melon we bought
into cubes, strawberry red. But they were
          dry, almost bitter.
     After the third taste, my father
dropped his fork. He gazed at the window
          for a while and spent
     the rest of his day in bed.

Before

Somewhere between faith and grace there is the footprint of logic lost in the purest light. Not hidden at all, but a vehicle, a necessity, neither mop, nor bucket, but whatever gives the floor its shine.

The sun through the window pours on the floor, and the wood glistens as if in praise. As if a child breaking into a run. That is what I see through the window now. A child breaking into a run for the simple flame that must burn and because there are such words as "snuffed out."

I could be wailing because the child is not a memory, only a gesture on my part. Yesterday, I fed a friend's cat and talked to her because the town has been emptied and filled with snow embroidered with tire tracks. I fed a friend's cat and she rubbed her sides against my calves. The thing to say now is that I am in the middle of a life in a house with the owners on holiday.

Or to say a car engine hums (the owner forgetting the keys inside) and is on its way to a crystalline loss. Here deduction is howling at an oncoming storm. The thing is, I fed a friend's cat and later poured a bowl of milk for her and she sniffed it, barely licked it, and left. The thought is. The life is.

I've visited graves—tombstones ten feet high. I ran through the cemetery and laughed my Cairo laugh. I wanted to be arrested by the police, wanted someone to take down what I had to say. Whatever I would have said would have been the truth.

But there was no one there. Only dust and a shitload of romance. Only dust and the dry tongue of the interstate. Detroit, Toledo, and the befores that follow the first before. Billions of snow flakes in between. I slam the brakes. I veer. The radio plays a Nigerian song. I feed the cat and talk to her and I take the milk away and begin to forget.

This was before. The first before. Days later I dissolve in the fumes of Houston. There are no snow flakes in Texas, and Muzak fills the emptiness in between. Your father died last week, I said. No one stares at the cat and the cat now stares at the missing bowl, and he stares at the after beyond before. Repeat after me. Repeat after me. A Nigerian song fills your town, fills the betweens with a billion befores.

Jeffrey McDaniel

Disasterology

The Badger is the thirteenth astrological sign.
My sign. The one the other signs evicted: unanimously.

So what?! Think I want to read about my future
in the newspaper next to the comics?

My third grade teacher told me I had no future.
I run through snow and turn around
just to make sure I've got a past.

My life's a chandelier dropped from an airplane.
I graduated first in my class from alibi school.

There ought to be a healthy family cage at the zoo,
or an open field, where I can lose my mother
as many times as I need.

When I get bored, I call the cops, tell them
there's a pervert peeking in my windows!
then I slip on a flimsy nightgown, go outside,
press my face against the glass and wait . . .

This makes me proud to be an American

where drunk drivers ought to wear necklaces
made from the spines of children they've run over.

I remember my face being invented
through a windshield.

All the wounds stitched with horsehair
so the scars galloped across my forehead.

I remember the hymns cherubs sang
in my bloodstream. The way even my shadow ached
when the chubby infants stopped.

I remember wishing I could be boiled like water
and made pure again. Desire
so real it could be outlined in chalk.

My eyes were the color of palm trees
in a hurricane. I'd wake up
and my id would start the day without me.

Somewhere a junkie fixes the hole in his arm
and a racing car zips around my halo.

A good God is hard to find.

Each morning I look in the mirror
and say *promise me something*
don't do the things I've done.

D

When the sun was a child's breath above the Earth
you were the one I turned to
wearing something dark and celestial
like the sky over Colorado.

You were elegant, like a night stick
balanced on the tip of a steeple

and seductive, like watching an archer
untie her bow.

You were the one I trotted to, like a horse
with a bell around my neck
and dangerous, like polishing the horn of a ram.

You rendered me crazy, like the footprints
of a husband chasing his wife
with a garage door opener through the snow.

You were mysterious, like a chandelier
suspended by a rattlesnake.

Your palms were the islands
of sleep I swam between.

A kiss with you was like driving off a cliff
clutching a sawed-off telescope.

When I split, pain spread through the rumor
of my body like the truth.

Knees turned to powder in their caps.

I rolled back and forth on the floor
like a four syllable word.

Every child I looked at
began coughing uncontrollably.

Every building I entered
became the house of separate beds.

Here is a bag filled with the vowels
that tumbled out of me.

Here is the sand castle I destroyed
with the limb of a friend.

Here is the sound of a hero
outgrowing his confetti.

Here, where the stars are scraps of metal
holding the world in place.

Following Her to Sleep

My friend wears boots to sleep
so I might learn her path.
I know the way now.

The room is as silent as a child in a closet.

I hang this notion from an instrument of hindsight
where it rocks at the appropriate moments like fortune's
cube on a string.

My neighbor with no arms wanted to know how it feels
to let something go.

I will need more than this map to get to sleep.

I tend the jonquils emerging from the volcanic
soil of her scalp.

A wave repeats itself in a bird cage.

I pay an elderly man to sit in a booth
and keep track of what crosses my mind:
a wedding where the only guests are former lovers
arranged by breast and penis size,
a doctor committing an emergency,
the echo of a silent *e*,
a plane always on the verge of landing.

Morale is down in the boneless
lactic fist of my genitals.

I cut my fingernails and glue them inside a diary
under the heading: definitive text.

Once I slept like a staircase in an abandoned home.
Now the shape of the body and the body
compete for the same seat.

Make each person's nose the size of their ignorance.

I am irresponsible. I lose the stars off my flag
which is invalid.

Turn on the lights and go to bed!

Check the bags under my eyes for explosives.

I sleep in separate beds.

Logic in the House of Sawed-Off Telescopes

I wanted to sniff the glue that holds families together.
I was a good boy once.
I listened with three ears.
When I didn't get what I wanted, I never cried.
I banged my head over and over on the kitchen floor.
I sat on a man's lap.
I took his words that tasted like candy.
I want to break something now.

I am the purple lips of a child throwing snowballs at a taxi.
There is an alligator in my closet.
If you make me mad, it will eat you.
I was a good boy once.
I had the most stars in the classroom.
My cheeks erupted with rubies.
I want to break something now.

My bedroom is so dark I feel like an astronaut.
I wish someone would come in and kiss me.
I was a good boy once.
The sweet smelling woman used to say that she loved me
and swing me in her arms like a chandelier.
I want to break something now.

My heart beats like the meanest kid on the school bus.
My brain tightens like a fist.
I was a good boy once.
I didn't steal that kid's homework.
I left a clump of spirit in its place.
I want to break something now.

I can multiply big numbers faster than you can.
I can beat men who smoke cigars at chess.
I was a good boy once.
I brushed my teeth and looked in the mirror.
My mouth was a brilliant wound.
Now it only feels good when it bleeds.

Campbell McGrath

The First Trimester

This morning we find dead earthworms in the dining room again.

Yesterday there were three; the day before one,

solitary traveller, lone pilgrim or pioneer shriveled up hard and black as the twist-tie I first mistook it for, shrunken and bloodless, brittle as wire.

Today it's two, a couple, bodies entwined in a death-embrace

become a cryptic glyph or sign, some Masonic rune or Buddhist talisman glimpsed in a Chinatown junk shop—

the ideogram of this mysterious manifestation.

So shall they come amongst us, singly and by pairs.

But where have they come from? The ficus? The yucca? A paltry crumbled trail of soil implicates the rubber tree, solemn in its dusty corner, in its green wicker basket among bookshelves. Is it possible? After all these years, how could it contain so much primordial, undomesticated life, so many wandering waves of worms? And what would induce them to leave it now, that safe haven of roots and humus, to migrate out into the great wide world, to wither and die in the vast dilapidated Sahara of our dining room floor?

Inseparable love? Biological compulsion? The change

of seasons? Autumn. Former students call

to speak of their suicides; the last yellow jackets

dive like enraged kamikazes to die enmeshed in our window screens, rusted auto-bodies awaiting the wrecker;

higher up, two geese,

vectored west against the contrails from O'Hare.

Last week two squirrels burst into my sister-in-law Becky's apartment and ran amok in a leaf storm of old mail and newspapers, chewing through a blueberry muffin and a box of Frango mints, whirling like the waters of the southern hemisphere counterclockwise around the living room until she chased them with a broom back out the open window.

From my window I watch the local squirrels settling in for the season, hoarding burrs and acorns and catkins, feathering their nest in the hollow limb of the big elm tree with insulation stolen by the mouthful from our attic.

At the church next door kids released early from evening service toss ping pong balls into colored buckets;

chimney swallows emerge from the unused smokestack that marks its former existence as a carriage factory to scour the dusk for insects, scattering and coalescing in fugitive rings,

coming together, breaking apart, coming together, breaking apart,

circling and circling in a sinuous wreath, ecstatic ash from the soul's bright burning.

Dusk: bicyclists; cricket chimes; the blue moon;

a single green planetary orb to grace the withered stalks of the tomato plants

in the garden. In the kitchen,

after removing the oatmeal raisin cookies to cool, Elizabeth has fallen asleep in the flour-dusted afterglow of baking,

in the sluice of pooled heat spilled like sugared lava from the oven,

in her clothes, on the floor,

sitting up.

Delphos, Ohio

is where we turned around, surrendered to fate, gave in to defeat and abandoned our journey at a town with three stoplights, one good mechanic and a name of possibly oracular significance.

Which is how we came to consider calling the baby Delphos.

Which is why we never made it to Pennsylvania, never arrived to help J. B. plant trees on the naked mountaintop he calls a farm, never hiked down the brush-choked trail for groceries in the gnomic hamlet of Mann's Choice, never hefted those truckloads of bundled bodies nor buried their delicate rootling toes in the ice and mud of rocky meadows.

Blue spruce, black walnut, white pine, silver maple.

And that name! Mann's Choice. Finger of individual will poked in the face of inexorable destiny.

Which is how we came to consider calling the baby Hamlet, Spruce or Pennsylvania.

But we didn't make it there. Never even got to Lima or Bucyrus, let alone Martin's Ferry, let alone West Virginia, let alone the Alleghenies tumbled across the state line like the worn-out molars of a broken-down plow horse munching grass in a hayfield along the slate grey Juniata.

Because the engine balked.

Because the shakes kicked in and grew like cornstalks hard as we tried to ignore them, as if we could push that battered blue Volvo across the wintry heart of the Midwest through sheer determination.

Which is foolish.

And the man in Delphos told us so.

Fuel injector, he says. Can't find even a spark plug for foreign cars in these parts. Nearest dealer would be Toledo or Columbus, or down the road in Fort Wayne.

Which is Indiana. Which is going backwards.

Which is why they drive Fords in Ohio.

Which is how we came to consider calling the baby Edsel, Henry, Pinto or Sparks.

Which is why we spent the last short hour of evening lurching and vibrating back through those prosperous bean fields just waiting for spring to burst the green-shingled barns of Van Wert County.

Which is how we came to consider calling the baby Verna, Daisy, Persephone or Soy.

By this time we're back on the freeway, bypassing beautiful downtown Fort Wayne in favor of the rain forest at Exit 11, such is the cognomen of this illuminated Babel, this litany, this sculptural aviary for neon birds, these towering aluminum and tungsten weeds,

bright names raised up like burning irons to brand their sign upon the heavens.

Exxon, Burger King, Budgetel, Super 8.

Which is how we came to consider calling the baby Bob Evans.

Which is how we came to consider calling the baby Big Boy, Wendy, Long John Silver, or Starvin' Marvin.

Which is how we came to salve our wounds by choosing a slightly better than average motel, and bringing in the Colonel to watch "Barnaby Jones" while Elizabeth passes out quick as you like

leaving me along with my thoughts and reruns

in the oversized bed of an antiseptic room on an anonymous strip of indistinguishable modules among the unzoned outskirts of a small midwestern city named for the Indian killer Mad Anthony Wayne.

Which is why I'm awake at 4 A.M. as the first trucks sheet their thunder down toward the interstate.

Which is when I feel my unborn child kick and roll within the belly of its sleeping mother, three heartbeats in two bodies, two bodies in one blanket, one perfect and inviolable will like a flower preparing to burst into bloom,

and its aurora lights the edge of the window like nothing I've ever seen.

Spring Comes to Chicago

All through those final, fitful weeks we walked off the restlessness of our daily expectancy on the avenues of sun-hunger and recalcitrant slush.

When would that big fat beautiful baby

blue first day of spring arrive?

So we strolled the backstreets and boulevards to consider the clouds and drink some decaf and escape the press of solicitous voices, gingerly, leaving feathers unruffled, like that first, fearless pair of mallards coasting the lake's archipelagoes of melting ice. We walked to the movies, again and again—Eddie Murphy at the Biograph, Orson Welles amid the Moorish splendor of the Music Box—varying our route until we knew every block in the neighborhood, every greystone and three-flat, every Sensei sushi bar and Michoaqueno flower stall.

We walked to Ho Wah Garden and the Ostoneria and over to Becky's for deep-dish pizza;

to Manny's for waffles on mornings of aluminum rain;

the German butcher for bratwurst, the Greek bakery for elephant ears, the 7-Eleven for cocktail onions to satisfy Elizabeth's idiosyncratic cravings.

We walked until our fears resurfaced and then we ate out fears.

We walked ourselves right out of winter into precincts we knew and those we didn't and some the city kept as private enclaves for itself, a certain statue, a street of saris, an oasis of cobbled lanes amid the welter of industry where suddenly the forsythia is in lightning-fierce flower, sudden as lilac, as bells, as thunder rolling in from the plains, sky a bruised melon spawning ocean-green hailstones to carry our rusted storm gutters away in an avalanche of kerneled ice plastered with bankrolls of last year's leaves.

Behold the daffodil, behold the crocus!

Behold the awakened, the reborn, the already onrushing furious and blooming:

violets overgrown in the lawn gone back to prairie,

some trumpet-flowered vine exuding sweet ichor upon the vacant house across the street,

dandelions blown to seed

and the ancient Japanese widows who stoop to gather their vinegar-bitter stems.

That final morning we clear the cobwebs and crack the storm windows to let the breeze take shelter in our closets and to bask all day in its muddy immutable odor. Elizabeth naps in a chair by the window, attuned to the ring of a distant carrillon, matins and lauds, while down the block an unnumbered hoard of rollerblades and bicycles propel their passengers like locusts assembled at the toll of some physiological clock, the ancient correlation of sap and sunlight, equinoctial sugar and blood. The big elm has begun its slow adumbration of fluted leaflets and buds on branch tips, percussive nubs and fine-veined tympani, a many-fingered symphony tuning up.

Vespers: swallows and doves;

Elizabeth takes a final stitch in her tiny welcome blanket; yawns; done.

Bodies and hours, bodies and hours.

At midnight I close the book on final grades to find my desk alive with a host of translucent, freshly-fledged spiders, a microscopic multitude borne in on the breeze to take up residence among the computer keys, a vision that bears me down the umbilicus of dreams toward a dim, persistent, unreasoning rhythm, a music long promised, a visitation at last given up and unlooked for, ghostly silk loomed from winter's cocoon or the opening of one wind-shaken blossom—

Behold the sleepers! When they wake everything,

o everything

shall be transformed.

Wheatfield Under Clouded Sky

Suppose Gauguin had never seen Tahiti. Suppose the *bêche-de-mer* and
  sandalwood trade had not materialized
and the Polynesian gods held fast in the fruit of Nuku Hiva and the milk-and-
  honey waters of Eiao.
Suppose that Europe during whichever century of its rise toward science had
  not lost faith in the soul.
Suppose the need for conquest had turned inward, as a hunger after clarity, a
  siege of the hidden fortress.
Suppose Gauguin had come instead to America. Suppose he left New York and
  traveled west by train
to the silver fields around Carson City where the water-shaped, salt-and-heart-
  colored rocks
appeased the painter's sensibility and the ghost-veined filaments called his
  banker's soul to roost.
Suppose he died there, in the collapse of his hand-tunneled mine shaft, buried
  beneath the rubble of desire.
Suppose we take Van Gogh as our model. Suppose we imagine him alone in
  the Dakotas,
subsisting on bulbs and tubers, sketching wildflowers and the sod huts of
  immigrants as he wanders,
an itinerant prairie mystic, like Johnny Appleseed. Suppose what consumes him
  is nothing so obvious as crows
or starlight, steeples, cypresses, pigment, absinthe, epilepsy, reapers or sowers or
  gleaners,
but is, like color, as absolute and bodiless as the far horizon, the journey toward
  purity of vision.
Suppose the pattern of wind in the grass could signify a deeper restlessness or
  the cries of land-locked gulls bespoke the democratic nature of our solitude.
Suppose the troubled clouds themselves were harbingers. Suppose the veil
  could be lifted.

HeidiLynn Nilsson

My Least Skirtable Deficiency

For the life
whose loss is less

articulate than its progress—
and for the pale, weightless

sorrow that enters,
scentlike—I should have

incessantly prayed.
Instead, I allowed

the wrong obsessions to be
always piloting

my prayers—the earth, the body's
generous affinities.

Last night,
even, I dreamed

it was noon at a shopping mall
where I was soon to be
executed. I prayed,

there, in my last living minutes,
that my body would fall
gracefully. I wanted to be

a lovely thing to look at—
like a fog descending—
composed, expressionless.

My omniscient God,
can you know
the sorrow of people

who forget to pray
for good life—
Can you know, Lord,

the sorrow
of people who can't,
at times, imagine

a section of themselves
that will not, however
gracefully, collapse?

On Inheriting Departure

It's easy for me to believe
that a woman, told not
to turn, would turn
to salt to see
her home burning.

You are, you could
convince me, my home.

A beautiful man is beautiful and a man
with ample sorrow also looks beautiful.
This is why it is best
not to look.

So I think of what
I am, what you are
leaving and

below, a child
pulls a lid and fireflies
fly out around him.

That's what my passions now
look like—like
that jar.

"We Are Easily Reduced"

—Franny Key

My groom, I fear, has grown
untidy. His litter now anticipates

my fixing—spits
of dinner chicken,

thunder in the coffee pot.
As said, my groom has grown

almost eight miles distant. Bending
toward a parade of vacated

shirts, shorts, warm
towels, I recall my mother

quick as an animal
gathering the touches

of my father—
boxers, breakfast dishes. Marriage

would fit differently
for us. Life would commence

tidily around us and between us
appetite, I thought.

Also I often
thought that to be spirit

which was heat only. Now
this affection reminds me

of Arizona—volcanic landforms,
intractable river

dammed. My mother sweeps
all day in my mind.

Canyons there
that can't be helped.

How Came What Came Alas

Came the hammer, so to speak,
the what had been,

for some time, coming. Came
unlike the wrath I had so often

fancied. Came frog song
over pains of open soil.

Came bird song over brimstone.
Came collected. Came prepared.

No one called, with any voice,
me close to it.

No lightning loud to lord
over—the meek lights

of longing only. Came seeming, to me,
at first, unlovely as afterbirth—

came lovely as the body butting
all that is unlovely out.

Come wild, I prayed, come
fire-like upon my undergrowth,

come like the halbert here
upon my candid breast.

But such as would be fit
for such a coming came said,

came weary of the wilderness,
came kennelled in my head.

Rick Noguchi

The Turn of Privacy

Kenji Takezo feels everybody
Watching him,
It is the biggest wave all day.
On a shortboard, he stands,
Cuts left.
Instead of doing the quick
Vertical maneuvers
Expected of him,
He borrows an old trick,
Makes it his.

He drops around his ankles
The trunks
His mother bought him
Last year for his birthday,
Exposing his private
Skin tone, the same color
Under his wristwatch.

The trunks at his ankles
Lose their purpose and become
Something else. Cuffs, binders,
Keeping his feet
Together, Siamese twins.
He cannot take the stance
Which would give him
The balance,
Enough to ride the wave's length.
He falls.

During the tumble, the wash of ocean,
The trunks are lost,
His feet twisting out of them,
Talents of an escape artist
He never practiced, never dreamed.
A sleight of hand, a sleight of foot,
That surprises him.

The crowd, laughing,
Waits to cheer him.
But Kenji stays in the shallows
Planning his next trick.
He makes the best of it,
Paddles back out,
Catches another wave, then another,
Until the crowd grows
Tired of him and forgets.

The Breath He Holds

It's the only thing Kenji Takezo does
Better than his brother Joe.
At last year's town competition
Kenji stayed under longest
Defeating Joe
And the six-year champ
Jack Sullivan who withdrew
After taking water in
Through the nose.

The family trophy case
Now displays the Steel Lung.
Kenji's the youngest
Ever to win it.
His parents are proud
He has such a knack,
That there is something
He can do besides surf.

To properly defend his title
This year, they purchase for him
A wooden vat,
Fix it in the rich soil
To stand near the older son's
Award-winning herb garden.
Hose water instead of wine
Fills it.

Kenji practices his technique
Back there twice a day
Before surfing and after school.
Saffron, sage, and basil
The last scents he breathes
Sinking down to sit
Cross-legged on the bottom,
A ten-pound brick in his lap.
Bubbles popping over his head,
No words inside them.
Nothing better on television
The neighbors come to watch him
Train until his skin becomes old.

I, the Neighbor Mr. Uskovich, Watch Every Morning Kenji Takezo Hold His Breath

Sometimes he will break
His concentration
And wave to me in a motion
Labored by water.
Bubbles, pouring out
His nostrils, much bigger
Than those in champagne
Opened to toast a new marriage.
He's only been under a few minutes
Today. I can't speak
Where he can see me,
Keep my thoughts to myself.

That Kenji cannot hear
The world, and the quick
Movement of lips
Frightens him.

The first time he saw
Someone speak
Words that weren't there,
He gasped
Inhaling his lungs full of water.
I was present when Mas,
The boy's father, found him.
He thought at first
His son was asleep,
Then that something was wrong.
He reached in hooking the boy
Under his arm to pull him from the vat.
But the fifteen-pound brick
That keeps Kenji submerged
Weighted him too well.

Mas in an act of love
Jumped in and lifted
His son high over his head.
I took the boy myself,
Carried him to the ground.
I put him in the basil plants.
Mas immediately started jabbing
His open palms into Kenji's belly
Driving out the water
That choked him.
In this way and on this morning
In this bed
He gave his son life.

The Really Long Ride

Kenji Takezo does not have the gift of vision
Except that in whatever he does see
He sees a wave. So when he walks
His way to school, he is surfing.

The row of houses surge into a wall of water.
He dodges the eaves crashing behind him,
Then ducks under the overhang of a tree,
The falling crest of a Pipeline breaker.

He stands beneath the shade where he hears
The hollow music inside the tube,
The green leaves shimmying like the ocean
Turning itself around him.

He exits the ceiling of foliage to outrun
The whitewash of cars chasing him.
Morning commuters showing all teeth and eyes.
Their blaring horns, fellow surfers cheering him on.

In this way, he surfs always.
His whole life, the longest ride,
The perfect wave in the ocean for which
He searches endlessly and never finds.

From Rooftops, Kenji Takezo Throws Himself

Be prepared
　　　　　　　—Boy Scout motto

In midair, he hesitates at the moment
Gravity begins its pull. Before closing
His eyes, he peeks at the earth
Spinning below him, wonders why
When he jumps into space
The planet never abandons him.

The trick, he must remember, is in the landing:
Keep his face and genitals out of it.
Adjusting himself in the air,
He arches his back and bends
His flailing arms and legs behind,
A broken swan plunging from the ten-foot heavens.
When he smacks the cool cement
Belly first, his heart bounces. Still, he holds
The wind, usually, inside him.

A year ago the ocean rose
Six feet before it turned and collapsed.
Tackled firmly, he saw nothing but white.
His belly slapped the sand.
His breath knocked free. Ten minutes
He struggled, floating without
Weight, until it was recovered
Safely from the grip of water.

To be certain he never again fumbles
The breath he has kept since birth
He rehearses the vertical flight
Every day, making his stomach strong.
Next week he will start
Leaping off two- and three-story buildings
Preparing for the wipeouts he will take
When he falls from waves
The size of cathedrals.

Kenji Takezo Becomes Water

The ocean with its large mouth swallowed him.
One bite, and very little chewing.
He balled up his body
As he sank into the belly,
Where the water waited to digest him.

He held himself together, his air
Kept tight, but the gas in his lungs began to expand.
It was choking
Him. He was choking himself.
So he gave up fighting back his breath,
His bubbles rose to the heavens.

The ocean burped,
A small disturbance on the surface.

Kenji relaxed his body, emptied
His thoughts into the element.
He became the ocean,
His mind and body floating with the current.
He no longer had to breathe.
When he opened his eyes,
He saw himself,
The deep blueness spanning the planet.

Barbara J. Orton

Love Poem

1

It wants to be dark, lavish
and exact: carved wet slate
bedded in an argument of peat.

With the precision of a fetishist
it fastens on detail: the thick veins
in your throat, the crooked line
of an eyebrow, the crook of an arm—

a tender dismemberment.
It wants to address one eccentric soul,
but always comes back to the physical.

2

It wants to be personal and minute,
but only pays its keep when it succumbs

to the universal: effacing the dear
Sir or Madam addressed,
it scatters its fondness to an audience.

The poem knows it is an act
of violence; and it resents the fact.

3

It is always, finally, about the *I*
and not the *you*. You are a dim
memory fleshed into the present tense.
You are my lover. You are a woman
I saw on the bus six months ago,
brushing her hair back with your hand.

You are my husband. Or you were.
You were a man before I changed your name.

4

Nothing I say will do you the least
atom of justice. Your hair

is very good hair and I like it.
You can read sheet music, and dissect
the workings of a microchip.
I admire that. Darling,

if somehow I could tell the exact truth,
all the girls would be after you.
Boys, too. Birds, plants. Even dining tables
would walk to your doorstep, hopeful, solemn,
with vases of peonies wobbling on their backs.

5

Or so I like to think. I'm not half
clever enough to chew out the trap
of the lyric—still, you're real enough,

for all this dithering. Yesterday
you stood on your doorstep with folded arms,
calling your dog: the self embodied
in that moment, a solid fact,

though even then I couldn't help
thinking of you as my favorite text,
thick and witty, in your leather vest.

Bacchanal

She boned three chickens—all except the wings—
and sat them on the counter in a row,
slouching like plump drunks, their arms around
each other's shoulders: at any moment
they looked as if they'd raise a hiccupy chorus.

A raw chicken's a stiff, awkward thing:
crossing its ankles, half-frozen inside,
a cage of bones aching to keep hold
of its neck and gizzard. But these three—
peeled away from their brittle wishbones
and the gristly propriety of a Pope's nose—

were like naked old men from Rubens.
Three loose bellies lolled over the splayed,
rubbery stubs of thighs. All they asked
was to be stuffed with chestnuts and red wine—
so given over to their helplessness
the dead flesh seemed to revel in its loss.

Beekeeper

The trick, he said, is to look not at all

like a bear. So, dressed in white—
the mild Italian bees having never seen
a polar bear—my father stole
nine combs of honey every fall.

He poured cedar smoke from a hinged
funnel like the Tin Woodsman's head:
the dizzy insects took his pale form
for a lilac bush or a cloud.

Once he wore dark socks by mistake:
the bees stung rings around his ankles.
Look, that bush has a beer hiding under it!
He called them his little suffragettes.

My treasure was the observation hive:
glass-walled, too small for harvesting.
With my palm on its warm flank
absorbing the hum of the collective,

I'd spend half an hour watching
their purposeful shimmy, the damp newborns
chewing out of their wax-capped cells
and fluttering wings like glass fans.

He showed me how to spot the queen among
the workers and the fat harmless drones
which would be calmly killed. When I came in
crying, with a lump under my foot,

he showed me how the dying bee had left
her gut strung to the barb in my sole.
Think about that, and stop howling,
he said, as he scratched out the sting.

I've seen him let a bee crawl on his finger
and carry her outside, and set her down
gently on the ragged grass. I've learned
to do that, as I've learned that honey

keeps for years, so intense it kills
the growth of things. Now I want to know
what I can keep of this, my father's
territory: the battered veil

and smoke, the white-painted hive
crackled and blurring into grey;
his precise habit, the stare
slicing edges, the words I choose,

my mouth like his, the old Orton
nerves pulling fractions of the past
into congruent cells; the black gleam
of honey, the slick white embryos

darkening into crumpled bees?

The Sea Monkeys

At first my mother balked I already had
two overfed gerbils, a tomcat I tried to dress
in baby clothes, guppies that kissed my fingers
and ate their young: what more
dominion could a girl ask for?
I pleaded, offered pocket money,
and at last I had it: a box
with a sheaf of directions, and three packets—
eggs, food, and salt broth.

As soon as they hatched, I knew
I'd been had. These were brine shrimp,
the kind that came with my microscope kit:
a quarter inch long, white,
brainless, spineless. All they did was twitch.

The next day I fed them to the guppies.
For years, I made do with dolls
and tractable playmates. It's just as well.
I don't like to think what would have happened
if, at that age, I'd had my heart's desire:
a colony of tiny human slaves.

Alan Michael Parker

Days like Prose

Epistemology, and all the afternoon
clouds perform their dying, tusks and trunks
dissolving in a rivulet of cold wind,

the sky a promise darkening.
Will it rain? The rain says it will
as thunder pools in every vowel,

beading in the wild raspberry patch.
Epistemology, and through the sliding
glass door of the moment

here is what I think: a man loves
being loved, shirtless on the lawn,
singing the song of a fat life,

of giddy children trampling the lavender.
I close my eyes as the red darkness
blooms inside, the sky recurring

just so—and deeper in the night
when the planes come out to fly,
their windows clean with dreams,

and the dead heroes jostle
in too-brilliant tombs, I shall sleep
the cool sleep of the unexamined,

and I shall pray the dizzying wheel
might spin again. Epistemology,
the evening mist sprawls in the grass,

the happy roaring dandelions
bow with dew. Here, I plan
to give up planning, watch the seagulls

dive for shiners in the foam
—where the neap tide unravels as
a warning buoy bobs beyond the known.

The Vandals

In the poem about the vandals, the vandals
Back their Dodge 4X4 up to the door

Of the abandoned town hall and theater.
In untied boots, they carry in their canvas bags

And carry off the oak wainscoting.
Above the wings and pit and stage, the ghosts

Of two starved porcupines command
Twin mounds of scat, respectively,

The prickly hats of king and fool.
(The chairs don't care, bottoms up, attentive.)

As the vandals stomp inoutinoutinoutinout
All in one breath because poetry

Is an oral tradition, the ghosts of the porcupines
Fill the air with rhyme: Visigoths and *mishegas*,

Gerkin and curtain, howitzers and trousers.
The vandals stomp inoutinoutinoutinout:

In their arms the split and pocked wood,
In their wake the porcupines

Are unaware of God's universal love.
In the poem, no one is free:

The ghosts of the two porcupines
Got in but they can't get out,

Starving over and over. The vandals—
Who sometimes look like you

And sometimes me—will never
Go home to cozy vandal homes

To make of their deeds a poem.
In the poem about the vandals,

Because a poem is an abandoned theater,
The porcupines have eaten the scenery:

Padua, Venice, Alexandria, Verona, gone;
Love prostrate on its pyramid.

And the vandals stomp inoutinoutinoutinout,
And the vandals stomp inoutinoutinoutinout.

Another Poem about the Vandals

In another poem about the vandals, the vandals
Toss their dullèd knives

Onto a table, scattering three hours' worth
Of peanut shells. A chant goes up:

More beer, more beer, more beer.
A barmaid waves, stubs out her cigarette—

Vaguely aware of
Waiting to die,

Restless in the blue TV light.
Separate checks, the vandals roar

In unison, as though they weren't
In a poem. The barmaid

Adjusts her bra, thinks about how pretty
Abstract Expressionism makes sorrow seem.

Where is that bitch, the vandals roar,
Just as the inexorable force of

History pushes her out into the snow:
More beer, more beer, more beer.

She has to try to quit the poem, and the vandals.
She closes the back door, glances toward

You and me—did she see us?—
And turns her collar up against the night.

Cruelty, the Vandals Say

Is learned. In this poem they're right,
Cold and huddled 'round a trashfire

Underneath the trestle bridge,
Hunger chewing on self-pity.

Look. Here comes the boy
Who will be your father,

A glass jar in a paper bag,
Holes jammed through the metal lid

To let a doomed toad breathe.
(The boy has your hands, your smile.)

Watch him leap the ties, counting
One-oh, two-oh, three-oh, here we go.

Smell the smell: ash and creosote.
(Why must the toad die? you ask.

Because the rhyme has told us so.)
The vandals clench their frozen fingers

Into fists, sing their vandal songs
Of switching yards, railway dicks, the moon

In strips across a lover's back
(On you, on me, on the

Everlasting). The boy unbends
A safety pin, says

Hey. C'mon. Wake up—
And skewers the toad. (Listen

For the whistle, the train
Is almost in the poem.)

And the vandals break into a howl
As the Limited roars o'er their heads

Like the very roar of Being;
And the boy hops off the tracks,

—He shall not die—
Unscrews the lid, shakes out the mess

(The toad, its soul, whatever.)
Oh, you say. Oh dear, oh me oh my.

The God of Pepper

In her best gingham dress, teased hair
And Odalisque #3, the God of Pepper

Descends, makes an entrance
Down the stairs

Into the church basement, one
Slender ankle then

Another
Slender

Ankle.
Pot luck! And hers is the Ambrosia,

The gelid, the burden
Of each twilight spent

Staring at the cupboard's contents,
All those tiny jars, so different.

(Hers is a love
Explosive, every moment

In her gaze
A long night and a short day.)

But now she has arrived:
She stands behind the table,

The supper laid
Like a Bingo card,

And gestures with an open palm
At all the offerings.

She smiles, never speaks, poses
Like a sculpture—a god in the finest

Old tradition—and then she leaves
In a cloud of suspicion and temptation:

A string of black pearls,
Inscrutable and good.

No Fool, the God of Salt

No fool, the God of Salt, beloved by all,
Has learned the difference between

Passing on and *passing through.*
She's been reading Einstein, once again,

To Solovine: "An infinite world is possible . . . ,"
Stoking herself on caffeine and Turkish Delight,

Feet in her square heels on a piano stool
In that little café off the Avenue.

You know the one? The Weimar?
Where once that tiny Lebanese chanteuse

Burst into flame? The God of Salt
Was there, as always, everywhere it seems,

But never much help,
Her minions stoic in their prisons,

Her skirt hiked up,
So many promises to break.

And the lovely singer caught, then sizzled,
Smoked, then raged, consumed.

The God of Salt? She looked up
From her book—as ever, Einstein,

"One should expect a chaotic world which cannot
Be grasped by the mind in any way . . ." —

And she licked her lips.
(Those lips, O, those lips.)

And she used the very pointed tip of her tongue.
(That tongue, O, that tongue.)

D. A. Powell

[nicholas the ridiculous: you will always be 27 and impossible. no more expectations]

nicholas the ridiculous: you will always be 27 and impossible. no more expectations

you didn't carry those who went in long cars after you. stacking lie upon lie as with children

swearing "no" to pain and "yes" to eternity. you would have been a bastard: told the truth

afternoons I knelt beside your hiding place. [this is the part where you speak to me from beyond]

and he walks with me and he talks with me. he tells me that I am his own. dammit

nothing. oh sure once in a while a dream. a half-instant. but you are no angel you are

repeating the same episodes: nick at night. tricky nick. nicholas at halloween a giant tampon

don't make me mature by myself: redundancy of losing common ground. for once be serious

[the thicknesses of victor decreased: blanket->sheet->floss. until no material would do]

the thicknesses of victor decreased: blanket->sheet->floss. until no material would do

in the shedding season: the few of us who had not turned had found his remote room in mercy

he wriggled slight as a silkworm on its mulberry bed. his lips spin slathering thread. he sleaved

we waited for his release and he was released: yellow and radiant mariposa. don't let us mend

[sleek mechanical dart: the syringe noses into the blue vein marking the target of me]

sleek mechanical dart: the syringe noses into the blue vein marking the target of me
haven't I always looked away. don't want to see what's inside me. inside me or coming out
older than balder: older than I'd planned to be. aliveness jars me. what's sticking what sticks

in my dream the haruspex examines my entrails. glyphs of the ancient chitterlings transcribed:
highballs. speedballs. chirujos. chickens. lues. spora. blasphemy. butter. bitters. epicac.
highrisk behavior posterchild: come reeve. a thousand happy tourists in-&-out me. I matterhorn

how much frivolity does the hypodermic draw away: does it taste men waferthin who blest my tongue
does it know knees I've dandled on. I feel taken in: darts in the waist of a coat I'll bury in

for I have husbanded recklessly: wedding daggers. holes in my memory of holes: danaidic vessels
the needle quivers. sickens. I spill names an alphabetsoup of hemoglobin. someone cracks the code

in a fortnight of waiting I draw up a will. develop false symptoms. how will I survive surviving

I'll throw parties where death blindfolded is spun: won't someone be stuck. and won't I be missed

[who won't praise green. each minute blade of spring. green slice us open]

a song of mayflies

who won't praise green. each minute to caress each minute blade of spring. green slice us

spew of willow crotch: we float upward a whirling chaff. sunlight sings in us *some glad morning*

when we are called we are called ephemera. palpitating length of a psalm. who isn't halfway gone

fatherless and childless: not a who will know us. dazzled afternoon won't we widow ourselves away

[sonnet]

a song of the big screen

morsels of my lifework: the story of a professional party hostess
I call this film "edge that can't know what I'm taking with me"
familiar and not shakespiliar. think *eurythmics* think *newamericanwriting*

a nice mix of plights and music. boomerang boy and disco dollies
I call this film "edge of a terrific current issue full of vice"
going to have witchdoctors in it. evil barbies. caymans and gators.

written in an enjoyable present: continuous. an unresolved work
I think I'll call it "edge literate and fresh and ugly." and "suitable?"
most of the shooting to be done in okinawa, okeechobee and omaha

most of the shooting nightlit super8 and under extreme conditions
roll credits: I call this film "edge that can't imagine how, given the situation"
suppose I'll be shopping for boots or intoxicants. props and settings

if you get my machine I'm on location: hazy hot humid. the far reaches
not to live mind you. to wrap up "edge where headed the winged cranes"

[darling can you kill me: with your mickeymouse pillows]

darling can you kill me: with your mickeymouse pillows
when I'm a meager man. with your exhaust and hose

could you put me out: when I'm a mite a splinter a grain
a tatter a snip a sliver a whit a tittle. habited by pain

would you bop me on the noggin: with a two by four
the trifle of me pissing myself. slobbering infantile: or

wheezing in an oxygen tent. won't you shut off the tank
mightn't you disconnect the plug: give the cord a proper yank

when I lose the feeling in my legs. when my hands won't grip
and I'm a thread a reed a wrack a ruin: of clap and flux and grippe

with your smack connections could you dose me. as I start my decline
would you put a bullet through me. angel: no light left that is mine

Claudia Rankine

Testimonial

*

As if I craved error, as if love were ahistorical,
I came to live in a country not at first my own
and here came to love a man not stopped by reticence.

And because it seemed right
love of this man would look like freedom,

the lone expanse of his back
would be found land, I turned,

as a brown field turns, suddenly grown green,
for this was the marriage waited for: the man
desiring as I, movement toward mindful and yet.

It was June, brilliant. The sun higher than God.

*

In this bed, a man on his back, his eyes graying blue.
It is hurricane season. Sparrows flying in, out the wind.
His lips receiving. He is a shore. The Atlantic rushing.
Clouds opening in the late June storm. This,
as before, in the embrace that takes all my heart.
Imagine his unshaven face, his untrimmed nails, as all

the hurt this world could give.

*

Gnaw. Zigzag. The end of the alphabet buckling floors.
How to come up?

The blue-crown motmot cannot negotiate narrow branches,
but then her wings give way, betray struggle,

intention broken off in puffy cumulus.
I wished him inside again.

Touched him. Feathery
was the refusal,

drawing together what thirsts. His whole self holding me in,
we slept on the edge of overrunning

———————————————————

with parakeets nesting
in porch lights and dying hibiscus covering the ground.

(a dry season choked in dust, etched cracks in dirt roads,
children down from the hills in the sweat of night

to steal water.

        Plastic containers in those hands,
over the gate to my house. I lie here, my head
on the prime minister's belly, listening: urgency
swallowed by worried stillness

enveloped again by movement, before, finally,
the outside tap turns tentatively on—

                *

Lower the lids and the mind swims out into
what is not madness, and still the body

                          feels small

against such flooding hurled through the dull and certain dawn.

You, you are defeat composed.

The atmosphere crippled brings you to your knees. You are
again where we find ourselves   dragged.
Your hand, that vagary in shadow.
So soon you were distanced from error. Nakedness
boiled down to gray days: hair in the drain, dead skin
dunning shower water. The morning cannot

be picked through, not be sorted out. Clearly, you know,
so say, This earth untouched is ruptured enough to grieve.

Matthew Rohrer

Brooklyn Bridge

Bowlegged lady crawled across the river on cables
and towers above me, sinuous stone lady.

Below me nothing but the two-inch dimension
of the two-by-fours, and birds bugging the barges.

Her Graceful pelvis arches into the orange evening,
implaccably. Who is she waiting for?

Precision German Craftsmanship

It was a good day and I was about to do something important
and good, but then I unscrewed the pen I was using
to see the ink. Precision German craftsmanship.
The Germans are so persnickety and precise,
they wash their driveways. Their mountains and streams
dance around each other in a clockwork, courtly imitation
of spring. They built the Panzer tank, out of rakes
hoses and garden gnomes; they built me.
And I've seated myself above an avenue on the brink
of mystery, always just on the lip, with my toes over the lip,
but my bowels behind.

When I replaced the ink the sky was socked in,
only one window of blue open in the north, directly over someone.
But that person was reading about Rosicrucians in the laundromat—
he was unaware as the blue window closed above him.
The rest of us are limp and damp.
I see a button in front of us that says "spin cycle."
I'm going to push it.

Gliding Toward the Lamps

The way a woman keeps her house
makes me want to sleep over
to see how she comports herself alone.

I see from across the street this woman likes to snuggle:
her alcove is smothered in comforters.
I imagine being curled up in there against the wall,
watching her tonguing a cruller.

As I glide home I think of the Robotroid Girlfriend,
and I am gliding toward the little lamps in her eyes.

I have turned her every-which-way and never
found the fuse box. I don't know how she works.
I think of the way she lies rumpled
in the rumpled bed, everything inside her switched on and purring.

I would love her bare arms to scissor my neck again.

The Hunger of the Lemur

On the hill he had climbed all winter
the lemur noticed a small black bird
with yellow spots,
the way the night ought to look.

The hill still slept under his feet
like something hard and dead,
it was the birds who were different.
The large black one, without confidence
now that the trees were softening
and the roofs warming up like pans.

A police car sighed with the contentment
of the overfed.
Burst chokeberries sat around
as reminders of death.
A girl stopped, then walked the other way.
The lemur couldn't smell anything besides himself
as if for the first time.
He thought:

I am a nose in a vacuum
shaped like a nose

I am the only lemur on the grey ice

These are only the slimy bones of trees,
not trees.

Ruth L. Schwartz

Why I Forgive My Younger Self Her Transgressions

Maybe it's the time I spend in high school classrooms
with the desperate loveliness
of all the young, the girls especially,
their damp, curled morning hair,
lips glossy and dark as rained-on plums.
I remember, at that age, dressing
to be visible,
penciling my eyes dark as a mockingbird's.
Everything was black, my nails, the velvet
choker looped around my neck,
and I made love like someone given
one day left to love, and lost, and blind

in the body's forest,
all that somersaulting thunder . . .
In time, a place transforms itself
through the quiet light of being seen.
Now the green evenings push through eucalyptus
branches, the trees shed their perfumed skins,
the weeks pass into months, scarcely
questioning themselves,
and everywhere the baby birds
still try to eat the universe,
all need, all stretched mouth like a skull,
saying *here, now*: this time, this place.

Falling in Love after Forty

Yes to the dark, uneven body of each tree
Yes to each blowing branch with its thousands of half-closed hands
Yes to the grass, its millions of wet and sentient blades
Yes to the gray-daubed sky above us and inside us
Yes to the headlights of oncoming cars, speeding brave unthinking,
      currents of white eyes
Yes to the red departing taillights, the rivers forming
      where they leave, the quiet which follows their rushing
Yes to the gravel driveways, the sweet, standing
      effort of the houses,
      the lights coming on in their windows the way a child
      opens her eyes after a long sleep, and, in the moment
      of waking, holds out her arms
Yes to the tiny rake spreading its rays around your eyes
Yes to the fields gone golden with dying
Yes to the ocean of light at the horizon
      under the electric wires, behind the rain

I don't want you young again, nor me
I want every sadness we've ever lived to stand here beside us,
      between the swaying soldiers of dead corn,
I want loss rolling around in our mouths
      where our tongues collide,
I want death sitting naked between us,
      lowering its head to lap at our champagne

Midnight Supper

Because nothing else can be done,
I peel the tough pale skin from the half-thawed
chicken with my bare hands,
the pink pulp of the meat between my cold
fingers, while the onions and cilantro,
the finely chopped bell peppers simmer
in coconut milk.

You said you wished you would die tonight.
This was after a long time of not speaking.
This was after you said you wished we could make love
the way we used to,
before the boulder of your illness
sunk us in our bed.
                    The sky was darkening; a ring of deep
orange glowed at the horizon,
the crickets were uninterruptable in their symphony,
and a slim scythe of a fingernail moon
had appeared, brilliantly,
and I tried to tell you I love you
like I love the world,
all that sunset and moon out there, and the hummingbirds
who come to drink their cherry-colored lives
from the feeder we hung,
and the shooting we hear every night,
the way the shots rise up through the air like furious
knocking on a door which will never be opened,
the sounds of people
killing people out there,
how I take all of it inside me, the whole bitter
shining landscape of our lives together.
I said to you over and over, I love you, until the words
were rain,
and I listened to the crickets, I watched the moon
as it took on more and more of the world's light,
becoming the only beacon of light, as everything else I could see
leached out its color into restive sleep,
and then, when you, too, were asleep,
I went down to the kitchen, to the kitchen
waiting clammily in its little foam tray, and began
to pull it apart.

AIDS Education, Seventh Grade

for M. M.

Day 1—AIDS Overview

The children are blooming like black flowers,
their teeth are white and lovely, it doesn't matter
what country they live in, the dying
moves over them like wind
through the captured fields.
When I ask how many know someone with AIDS
they all shout, their arms rising like snakes,
waving hungry palms,
can a dog get it, can you get it from a hickey,
did it come from red monkeys,
why can't they just pump out all a person's blood
and put in new?
Afterward the teacher says to me, That one there,
buck teeth, she has sex with three or four boys a week,
they come over from the high school,
do it to her in the yard,
her sister had a baby at thirteen—

                                    and overhead, the dark
bodies of the hawks
riding their hunger through the clear sky,
the sun laying its fair, long tongue
over everything.

Day 2—A Speaker with AIDS

One-third of the class speaks no English
And Mark of the beautiful Indian cheekbones,
the barrio, the broken, winged life
stumbles in his grandparents' Spanish
so the solemn little freckled kid translates
as Mark says, Tell them it's going to kill me,

This poem follows the sequence of the three-day AIDS education program provided in many Bay Area schools.

saying, *Dice que lo va a matar,*
his dark-lashed sunflower face composed

and the sun says, Forget about the forty days
and nights of rain, I'm here, I'm burning

    Day 3 — You Must Protect Yourself

It's like shouting from the shore
of a glittering lake,
Look, we've been given these bodies
we don't understand,
we could spend our whole lives
learning how to live in them.

It doesn't matter what I say.

Sex, if it hasn't already, will rise up in them
like something from another world,
like the snowy egret on its perfect stilts
in the dank puddle by the highway
shocking in its grace,
fishing for its life.

Angela Shaw

Crepuscule

Yellows cast their spells: the evening primrose
shudders unclosed, sells itself to the sphinx
moth's length of tongue. Again a lackluster
husband doesn't show. A little missus

eases the burnt suffering of a cat-
fish supper, undresses, slowly lowers
into a lukewarm tub. In her honeymoon
nightgown she rolls her own from the blue

can of Bugler, her lust a lamp the wick
of which is dipped in sloe gin. Hands
wander to her hangdog breasts, jaded Friday night
underpants, hackneyed nylon in heat.

Now his black taxidermy outstares her, the stern
heads of squirrel and deer. Now the house confesses,
discloses her like a rumor, vague and misquoted.
From the porch, from the glider she spies rose-

pink twilight flyers—sphinx moths drinking
the calyx, the corolla, the stamen
dry. The stuttering wings, the spread petals
suggest an interlingual breathing, a beating

back of all false tongues. She thinks of the chaw
lodged in his lip when he talks or her husband's
middle finger in the snuffbox and rubbed
along his gum. She walks, wanting him, into the latter-

math, into the primrose, the parched field itching
with critters. She walks, wanting and unwanting
him while birds miss curfew into the thick of the thigh-
high grass, craven and dangerous, in the heavy red.

Rear Window

for Grace Kelly

Love is a hovering, a deafening
batting of lashes. It presses

its lips to the opaque
blotting paper before breaking
and entering—a vision

suspended in moonlight, a museum

piece, a nude

summer hue. Love's petal-
starched dresses rustle in the under-
brush; its white cotton gloves

erase their own incriminating
traces. A lady

keeps her suitor guessing.

No matter the apparatus:
a handbag, a snifter, a pinch
in his drink,

a cinch

at the waist, an intellect trimmed
like a smart pillbox hat.
A lady proposes

a dangerous abetting
and proves her authenticity
by how easily

she bruises. Love is a cut-
up, a close-up,

a hovering.
This kiss is exquisitely
scripted and its twin

is terror.

April

is all laze and boudoir. She reclines, wigless
and half-naked in the haze of her private
rooms, chain smoking, deflowering éclair
with furtive tongue, bemoaning the pinch
of her little miss shoes. She is more freckled
than is suspected, less young, and when the mouth
of her silk robe unfolds it confesses
her dimpled skin, the lap of rich thigh
on rich thigh. She jiggles her clinky
bottles, sips at her tinctures, weeping
easily over this hidden toilette: burnt
curl, slipped hem, the short, huffy cough
of powder puff. Her muttered curses are coarse
as grosgrain as she totters in corset
and stockings, rehearsing protocol, her self-
mocking curtsy. But she clears like water and later
will deny you saw her or knew her as she
litters with lipstick imprints spring's cotillion.

Bird Nests

The year dead-ends here. Clumsy December
stubs itself against its own rigid house-
keeping, spare and disaligned, nothing where
we remember it. Today a new word
grows into our easy speech: thermostat,
oatmeal, *tumor*, bedtime. Wise to the sun's

ruse we find laughable each half-assed try
at rising, at meridian. Now near
dusk we walk where the jagged lake grates
on the injured grass. Some sickness quickens
in you or what the doctors, those wordsmiths,
call *growth*. Beyond the house our great oak pumps
in the wind like a wild lung. Dumb earth.
The tap root's hit concrete and the sap won't
give. The evening sky silhouettes dark clots
of hair and straw, pilfered bits of thicket
caught in branches. Somebody lived here once.
Your X-ray haunts, the way they all badmouth
your chances, and the *spot* we're told to *watch
closely* like some rare species that may take
wing, flighty and blind, slowly spreading south.

Small Pleasures

The wurlitzer stirs, all girl, all groan
and moment, everything pretty
hesitance

and pregnancy. Little furls
of lipstick, little wiles, sausage
curls beguile the makeshift

dusk, the boys, their pretty head-
over-heels makeshaft liftoff.
Laughter curdles in the throats

and limbs of late
april magnolia. A tree full of pink
wishes, each bud clenched

in its private
tantrum. Other petals spin
a tarantella: kleenexes

and kleenexes dropped in approximate
ladylike gesture.
On a high stool a lady or high

school girl tipples and swithers,
all purr and murmur, working
her clumsy rosary of car

keys and house keys, making the dim
room do her fast
dancing. Elsewhere, cypriniform

fishes suck at the rough
creek bottom, muttering
leftovers, leftovers.

In the backwater catholic
pucelles swelter
in their lycra-spandex sunday

dresses,
all prayer and murmur, lip-
synching *my soul*

is thirsty for you O Lord,
and the bored organist kindles his bored
organ

for the misses, dizzy
with jesus and little visions
of their own late-night

acts of mercy. The brimstone
boy, his mason jar full of snarling
bees, wades into the soft-core

porn of moths where they wallow
and dissolve in the dogbane,
knees and faces

glazed with pollen.
Nightly birdsong,
boozy

and uvular, suggests the indelicate
question
would she let her Texas

blues infect my red,
her wily
silences potent as jukebox

promises
in the low
dusk of the bowling alley

where the wurlitzer
stirs, all girl, letting Motown
down easy.

Reginald Shepherd

The Difficult Music

I started to write a song about love, then I decided, *No.*
I've been trying to write about violence
for so long. (You were my mother; I love you more
dead. Not a day goes by when I'm not turning someone
into you.) A week of traffic jams and fog
filtered through glass, the country crumbling
in my sleep; old men in plaid jackets on the corner
drinking quart bottles of Old Milwaukee; the color black
again and again.
        My first summer in Boston
a bum glanced up from tapping at the pavement with a hammer
to whisper *Nigger*, laughing, when I walked by.
I'd passed the age of consent, I suppose;
my body was never clean again. In Buffalo a billboard
said, "In a dream you saw a way to survive and woke up
happy," justice talking to the sidewalk on Main Street;
I thought it was talking to me, but it was just
art. (I've wronged too many mornings hallucinating
your voice, too drunk with sleep to understand
the words.)
        Some afternoons
I can see through a history of heart attacks in two-room
tenement apartments, writing your silted name
on snow with which the lake effect shrouds
a half-abandoned rust belt city. (I've compared you
to snow's unlikely predicates, the moon's
faceless occupation. Some drift
always takes your place.) I was just
scribbling again. *Take it from me*, my stereo claims, *some day*
we'll all be free. If anyone should ever write that song.
The finely sifted light falls down.

Another Version of an Ocean

You dreamed of drowning there, but couldn't read
the platitudes erosion wrote with sand. High tide
burned up the light, spray left you blind to every line
that leads a horse to water and makes him drink

the salt. You wanted to know why a cup of ocean
sluiced down a waiting throat would parch
the irrigated flesh, why sharks have to keep moving, stalking
oxygen. Like you waking to morning blinking fitfully

through plastic blinds, palm fronds, at sea no farther out
than anyone, they are too restless to be held
in those clean waters and preserved. They can't be still there
and still breathe, the body finding its own level

like any water. That was over your head.
There was something else you wanted from the light, whiter
than salt boiling to foam and glistening as error. Gulls
staggered across fractal clouds, drunk

on any prevailing draft. You combed the crumbling dunes
for desiccated sand dollars and doubloons, driftglass
rubbed down to amber, tiger's eye and jade: found only
crumpled styrofoam and paper cups, castaway's note

crammed in a green wine bottle, tossed into a blue garbage can
instead of cursive whitecaps. It might as well have been a beach.
I saw you there. Here's sand to fit your eye, here's a
salt rose, kelp rope, pearled abalone shell, turbinate

purple whelks and, far out, something
swimming into evening light laid on the sea to dry.

Motive

I'm a penny fallen from heaven's
corner pocket, anybody's overcoat, pick me up
and I'll bring you all kinds of luck. I'm a fence
burning down, love locked in a box, I'm a map

of hand-me-down tomorrows, the last
but one, or anywhere you never wanted
to go, but now. I'm a clock without a face,
I'm blind like time, so lead me on: wear me

on your wrist and I'll tell you things
you might not know, secrets spilled
like a rain forecast. I'm a cup you can
drink me from, cut glass and lucid

distortion, I'm solid water shattering
in hand, or daylight on a midnight
lake. *Remains* is what remains
of this, ambiguous number and tense

as any departure, all impossibility collected
for your sake. Greenhouse, little summer
under winter's latinate lattice of stars,
early or old snow, you're the reason

inside things, sheer likelihood: sense of speed
in the always almost here, the whitedark justice of us.

The Gods at Three A.M.

The foolish gods are doing poppers while they sing along,
they're taking off their white t-shirts and wiping the sweat
from their foreheads with them, the gods have tattoos
of bleeding roses on their shoulders, perhaps a pink triangle
above the left nipple, for them there's hope. The gods

are pausing to light cigarettes while they dance, they're laughing
and sharing private jokes while the smoke machine comes on,
one of the gods told you they put talcum powder
in the artificial fog, then walked away, how could anyone
breathe talcum powder, but it makes their skin shine
with the sweat and smell of cigarettes and Obsession. Don't try
to say you didn't know the gods are always white, the statues
told you that. The gods don't say hello, and when you ask them
how they are the gods say they don't know, the gods
are drunk and don't feel like talking now, but you
can touch their muscled backs when they pass.

The gods in backwards baseball caps say
free love, they say *this is the time*, and disappear
into another corner of the bar, they're always moving
to another song. The gods with their checked flannel
shirts unbuttoned under open motorcycle jackets,
hard nipples and ghost-white briefs above the waistbands
of their baggy jeans, say *get here*, the gods say *soon*, and you just
keep dancing because you don't know the words, you hope
the gods will notice small devotions and smile, maybe
a quick thumbs-up if you're good. The gods
whose perfect instances of bodies last only
for the instant, or until last call (and then
they disappear into the sidewalk), gods who are splendid
without meaning to be, who do they need
to impress, say *this could be the magic*, they say
live for tonight, and then the lights come on.

Larissa Szporluk

Holy Ghost

All my thoughts of you are good ones.
The horse whose neck is clothed with thunder—
they are good ones.
*The voice that shakes the wilderness—*good ones.
I think about how, if I could wake up,
I could go to your life,
how that would be good, if I could wake up.

But where I am is so large.
You are a fly.
You are impossible.

Where I am is so large, like a dark saying,
repeating. Where I am
is repeating. I don't know where it begins.

Where I am is the same.
but the light just takes you away, and I
am the only one here.
It's mine, like a dark saying—
Hide them in the dust together.

Bind their faces in secret.
You see how it's mine? You see how I try
to wake up?
The horse whose neck is clothed with thunder—
they were good ones.

I am the only one here, a giant,
asleep on the damp floor.
I am on the floor
of my invention, my forest
of dark sayings—
the Lord shall hiss.

My forest is always the same.
I am asleep on the damp floor.
My lids are down. Your face is a secret.
Hiss, hiss.

Triage

When there is no more life,
step outside. Peel away the human.

If the sky can't keep an opening,
be the opening

that ushers in the dusk
that masquerades the nothingness

with arteries of color,
the swell and swerve of nervous

wrecks, their kamikaze
shadows. Be that symbol

of the lost but well-fought war,
the bandage on the side effect,

not the real sore, of thousand-mile
bitternesses crossed by geese

against the odds of snow
until what binds them to repeat

themselves dissolves,
muscles, wings and throats

twisting like grotesques
of ice, their inner water, in a flux,

indentured to the half
they didn't know, like galaxies,

accessories, before the fact,
drawn into the power of a hole.

Axiom of Maria

Clover fills the darkness quickly,
splitting open, spreading.

It's a slightly different planet
that surrounds the same night,

an unction in the sun
that spins the Earth faster—

the couple pulls apart, turning hostile,
her body taking off into the wild,

his influence inside her
showing like a stripe, the same question,

Where is my palace, asked of the mountains
beyond her dream, as if time

were on fire, peregrines, herons,
burning in everything, singed by need,

as if all the metals in the world
surfaced, blowing out of people,

carbon, sulphur, gold—
the feeling she had had while climbing

was a feeling of being alloyed
with a shrinking attraction to life,

like a child suddenly old, a feeling of being
the greatest voice as it ceased,

rain hissing through her, a blue comet,
coming and going in streaks.

Occupant of the House

Someday the phoebe bird will sing.
The sword grass will rise like corn.
I will be free and not know from what.
Like a pure wild race
captured for science, too wronged
to go back, too strange to be damaged,
my fierceness has disappeared.
If it doesn't end soon, the pain will dilute,
the sin turn to sheen in the garden,
your routine a genial rain.
And I would get up from my special chair
and swim through the soundproof ceiling,
its material soft and blue,
a threshold to mobile worlds.
I wouldn't know about my body.
If it were winter, winter would tingle,
summer would burn,
like the lamp in my ear that bristles like fire
when you examine the drum—
is it hot? *I don't know.*
A shell malnourished by darkness,
a great fish charmed into injury, I swallow
the wires, the hours, the shock.
You knew what the sky would mean to me.

Ann Townsend

Mardi Gras Premortem

The good times were drunk times,
when your body loosened to a soft chair
and you closed your eyes. Or when we'd rove
bar to bar, clutching cold drinks, out onto
the cobbled streets, our plastic neon go-cups
shaking with ice. We jostled through a holiday crowd,
mummers hurled beads at our feet, the women
on the balconies lifted their shirts
for a handful of coins or souvenir mugs,
for three cheers, for more beer.
Sometimes there was caviar in gold cups;
sometimes your cigarette set the sofa afire —
and when, driving home, the car skidded
lovingly against the bridge's steel girder,
we were still happy drunks, who never saw
the blood, the shattered glass at our feet.

First Death

The first pains came slow,
    careful needle threading cloth;
        then the chronology of labor's absolute path.

She let the doctor, sweat-smeared angel of light,
    ease her. He cupped the plastic mask
        across her face and when she woke

alone in blood-streaked sheets,
    the boy was gone from her body.
        She never spoke the word.

There were others: *the great reward,*
     passing on, sleeping peaceful
          in the light. Not a good baby,

the doctor said.
     Nurses bound his head
          in careful wrappers, so she did not see

the fistula, the open spine.
     Wheeled to a window, she saw from a distance
          how the baby slept, or seemed to sleep.

But herself, she lived,
     and later years there were others:
          living children followed,

fat, healthy, heads full of hair.
     She kept no diary, she kept no record.
          Even the grave was lost in water-marked files.

But every night, brushing sparks
     from their fine, wild hair,
          she cupped the solid mass of each one's skull,

its declivities, its secret provinces,
     its skin and hair grown out of nakedness
          toward joy. And that was her sorrow.

The Bicycle Racers

Daredevil riding on the concrete lip
of an unfilled swimming pool, my brother
cartwheeled into the deep end,
tumbling twelve feet onto blue tile:

1969. Our parents disappeared.
We wandered loose, mining the woods
for the snake coiled underfoot,
lost dog shot between the eyes, for the farmer

who loved an audience while he beheaded
chickens for the church dinner.
Where were they when his birds fell
in a shower of blood, slavering their spattered wings

into the dust of the farmyard? Where were they
when I grew up wild?
I trust the blanket of solitude.
Now, when my daughter

prefers my company over her books
and a thousand piecemeal plastic toys,
I set her on her bike and push her free,
toward the narrow gravel road.

Ten stitches to the lip and a mangled
front tire: my brother lay there
for an hour moaning before the dogs
found him, and set to barking.

Purple Loosestrife

is too good to be true, in all its definitions.
Once beloved, once beautiful: today the wildflower magazines
apologize for including it. It induces wrath
in water-gardeners everywhere. Crews of volunteers
uproot and burn the plants from marshes in Minnesota.

Like the remedies of revisionists, it does the job
too well—like kudzu, or hybrid trout, anything introduced
with good intentions. It wipes out the competition.
Where it grows best it is least desired.
You can't buy it in any nursery.

Doing its enterprising best it seeds itself,
driving out local weedy growth, what fits, what came first.
Best-named of all wild things, for those who love the names,
it casts itself into the swamps and will not quit.
Like an imperialist, it has changed the landscape forever.

Rouge

That morning she stood in the kitchen
and considered the chair, its ignoble lines,

its wood of no interest or value, no grain
to coax out with a brush, no grace to enhance

with the tools one uses to strip away old varnish.
So she bought a can of spray paint,

thinking, I'll just cover it up.
She laid newspaper onto the clean linoleum.

She crouched beside the chair and worked
from the legs up. She thought she was a genius—

the paint swirled around the chair and settled
without streaks. Cherry red, barn red,

razzle red. Blood red as the thin spray floated
in the soft air. Only day by day,

as the chair hardened in its new skin,
as she cooked the same indifferent meals,

did she see the wash of color she had cast over the room.
Lit by a deeper light, one grade darker shadow,

the kitchen reddened, as if it had been pollinated
by the most wrathful tropical flower.

It came off on her fingertips, on the sponge
she drew across the counter. And the white stove

held the shadow of the chair across its hinged door
like a photographic negative, or the silhouettes

of the dead on the late night detective movies,
drawn on the floor where they fall.

Natasha Trethewey

Naola Beauty Academy, New Orleans, Louisiana 1943

Made hair? The girls here
put a press on your head
last two weeks. No naps.

They learning. See the basins?
This where we wash. Yeah,
it's hot. July jam.

Stove always on. Keep the combs
hot. Lee and Ida bumping hair
right now. Best two.

Ida got a natural touch.
Don't burn nobody.
Her own's a righteous mass.

Lee, now she used to sew.
Her fingers steady
from them tiny needles.

She can fix some bad hair.
Look how she lay them waves.
Light, slight and polite.

Not a one out of place.

Bellocq's Ophelia

—from a photograph, circa 1912

In Millais' painting, Ophelia dies face up,
eyes and mouth open as if caught in the gasp
of her last word or breath, flowers and reeds
growing out of the pond, floating on the surface
around her. The young woman who posed
lay in a bath for hours, shivering,
catching cold—perhaps imagining fish
tangling in her hair or nibbling a dark mole
raised upon her white skin. Ophelia's final gaze
aims skyward, her palms curling open
as if she's just said *take me*.

I think of her when I see Bellocq's photograph—
a woman posed on a wicker divan, her hair
spilling over. Around her, flowers—
on a pillow, on a thick carpet. Even
the ravages of this old photograph
bloom like water lilies across her thigh.
How long did she hold there, this other
Ophelia, nameless inmate of Storyville,
naked, her nipples offered up hard and cold?

The small mound of her belly, the pale hair
of her pubis—these things—her body
there for the taking. But in her face, a dare.
Staring into the camera, she seems to pull
all movement from her slender limbs
and hold it in her heavy-lidded eyes.
Her body limp as dead Ophelia's,
her lips poised to open, to speak.

Photograph of a Bawd Drinking Raleigh Rye

Storyville, 1912

The glass in her hand is the only thing moving—
too fast for the camera—caught in the blur of motion.

She raises it, a toast she offers the thirsty viewer
you become, taking her in—your eyes starting low,

at her feet, and following those striped stockings like roads,
traveling the length of her calves and thighs. Up then,

to the fringed scarf draping her breasts, the heart
locket, her bare shoulder and the flash of dark hair

beneath her arm, the round innocence of her cheeks
and Gibson-girl hair. Then over to the trinkets on the table

beside her: a clock; tiny feather-backed rocking chairs poised
to move with the slightest wind or breath; the ebony statuette

of a woman, her arms stretched above her head. Even
the bottle of rye is a woman's slender torso and round hips.

On the wall behind her, the image again—women in paintings,
in photographs and carved in relief on an oval plane.

And there, on the surface of it all, a thumbprint—perhaps
yours? It's easy to see this is all about desire, how it recurs—

each time you look, it's the same moment,
the hands on the clock still locked at high noon.

Cameo

As a child, I would awaken dark mornings
to peer from beneath the bedcovers and watch
my mother dress. She'd perch on a stool
at the cluttered vanity. Under the oil lamp

golden tubes of lipstick and atomizers glowing
like bottled light. She wore a pale slip, clinging
like water to her back. I'd watch her lean in close,
plucking the small hairs at her brow into points

that aimed down toward the corners of her mouth.
Her dress hung on the closet door as if
after mastectomy, the bodice empty
where her breasts would push against the fabric,

perfume heavy even after dry-cleaning—
the warm scent of her body filling the tiny room.
Before she'd move away from the mirror,
my mother would tie on a black velvet ribbon

at the back of her neck, so tight it seemed to hold
her together, the fine bones of her neck in place.
In the front, a cameo pressing into the hollow
of her throat, hard enough to bruise.

Karen Volkman

Daffodils

Oh my mimics, my gangly girls,
morning came quickly
with blushes and exits,

you left without saying
goodbye, without warning, Sonia
and Nina, by moonlight leaping

white steps to the station, Nina
and Anya, you left
no addresses, pointe shoes

in your handbags, lipstick askew,
Anya, Maria, the conductor called
Dreaming, the conductor called *Dancing,*

the conductor called *Far,*
you saw towers and bridges, Maria
and Katya, horizons and oceans,

gowns and perfumes
(by moonlight leaping
white steps to the station), dear Katya,

Marina, you left no addresses,
no notes or instructions,
no map and no route, the conductor

called *Farther,* and we gaze
from the platform, to your pale eyes,
Marina, Sophia, on the train.

Shipwreck Poem

I

Navigation's gone haywire. Who's to blame?
Night blacker than chartless depth

and above us
the astonishing unimpeachable stars!

and pale my sister
votive Pole Star, oracular tear.

In no dream of safety
do we live—bed and wave—

as I lost faith to be here.
It was love that shattered my compass—

searching room to room in the storm,
and you gone, the new moon

blind with delusions, the high deck
reeking of whale oil and tallow,

imagined latitudes,
instruments and digits,

the mast splintered
in a rogue wave, the flotsam crying

This is the life you made.

II

The sea deposits debris
carelessly, as though it could be

the whole story, clue held
to eye to tongue to ear,

wonderful offal! Ungraspable,
the whole deep havoc

adheres to the hands of the Collector,
who would be clear

as shore lights in summer.
What I left to be here—

certain firmament and fair wind,
for spiky trophies and

attenuating shore.
O lord I spoke too soon

of love and the wondrous.
Outside my skin it was always

bad religion.
The same story:

a child's yellow shovel
and a world to dig in.

Clear as shore lights in summer,
forward not back

swims the woman
I *will* be, summoned

not with the compass, *not* with the map.

Untitled

Shrewd star, who crudes our naming: you should be flame. Should be
everyone's makeshift measure, rife with tending—constellations called *Scatter* or
Spent Memory or *Crown of Yes* or *Three Maids Slow in Pleasure*. Some days my
eyes are green like verdigris, or green like verdant ardor, or like impair. Does it

matter the law is a frame to hang your heart in? This *was*. I saw it, schemed it, bled it. I was *then*. Or: I ran with all my leagues of forgotten steps to reach you. A rose said to a rumor, is fame what blooms with flanged petals, or is that cause? Are blind bones brighter in skulled winter or spring-a-dazing? I am asking the most edgeless questions, so words will keep them, so the green gods in my mind will lull and lie. But constellation *Mute Cyclops*, my ravaged child, weeps every eye.

Untitled

I won't go in today, I'll stay out today. I won't go home today, instead I'll go to sea. Today is a lot of work, yesterday wiser. Yesterday is a path made out of feet, today is a screwball alarmclock with a mawkish tick. Today offends everyone with nebulous gesture: "I think." "Yes but." "Still really." "Gee well." This becomes language you know becomes destiny, still you know that operator listening in on the phone? She of the darker stare and windy grimace? Yes she is writing every word, I wouldn't leave that blur too conspicuous, knapsack of roar. I wouldn't give just anyone access, but you know best. Seems to me you go out a little too spryly, hardly a step really more of a *sprawl*. You packed your bags reasonably enough, but what about all that dubious baggage from last fall? Seems we're in for shriller weather, your eye no more mild decries tornado and scar. Today needs a few more devotees lacking grace. But yesterday, imperious echo, knows who you are.

Untitled

We did things more dulcet, more marionette. There were equivocations— usual modems—all sorts of agos. Then—in time—the needed accretion.

How much like a star we were, light as blazons. Nomad of a thousand paths, surely there are tempers more like yours, acrid and fulsome, whose articulated measure is a queenly Entire. Then we counted our fingerprinted petals—kept dryer in a pale tin—rose and carnation—loved, attended, tamed.

Be attention, dear border, you wander too far. Your music is dissonant sometimes, calamitous fugues and fallow, echoed tones, you are turning too many melodies into maunder. It seems we are creature, we devour and leave.

But when late light turns the leaves gold, when the red pine offers its armfuls of snow, we are not hunger and perjure. In that moment (blemish and blossom) we are *gaze*.

Rachel Wetzsteon

Urban Gallery

When the wind invades the treetops
and the trees agree, shivering
take me, take me, when their
stealthy perfume drifts down to waft
among mortals, they come out in droves:
the boy whose bouncing keys speak a language
all their own, the novice who gets her tricks
from magazine molls (their haughtiness, swirl
of cleats), the gigolo with eyes lowered,
the better to judge his prey, the woman
whose hemlines rise as her age does,
the bad girl whose only remaining option
is to get worse: despite the string of cheats
and lukewarm reactions, she still has
the power to pound, the knack of
funneling her frustration into
the arrogant click of a heel . . .
at this armada of proud, unyielding soldiers
I have cast ferocious stones, holding forth
on barricaded gardens and souls' communion
until, heaving my bones from garret to gutter
I took to the street and saw it, too, was worthy.
Chasers out for a good time, flirters in
for a life's catch, strutters so skilled your
lurid designs burn holes, kill the cold
in the pavement, it does not matter
what fever you feed, so long as
you feed it freely; I hid my eyes
but sickness is catching; lovers, permit me entrance.

Drinks in the Town Square

No sooner had they carried their martinis
over to the café's remotest table
and huddled close to praise the coming sunset,
red as a famous letter, than it happened:
empty when they had entered it, the square now
quivered with life. What she saw: burly spinsters,
big books in hand, refusing to be selfless,
women in white and, lurking in the shadows,
elegant lady spies. What he saw: strutting
romeos, hearts for rent, devoted scholars
for whom high windows could outshine rich widows,
cynics for whom all cities were the same.
They had come all this way, by plane, by marriage,
hoping to pit their love—with all its thriving,
colorful avenues, unending crops—to
everything else, but now the square was teeming
with all the faces they had left behind!
Visitors from their own obstructed futures
dazzled their eyes and scarred their hearts much more than
glamorous strangers they could never have,
and when the square began to reassemble
they butted heads and called each other darling,
as if to cover private crimes with public
blandishments. But there was no denying
that each grinning face was a murderer.
When all the ghosts got up and walked out, they were
left with a vivid sense of screen doors closing,
and when they staggered homeward, there were trembling
fists in their pockets, daggers in their eyes.

A Rival

Names flow from her mouth as so many hearty allies;
she's breezy host to a horde of stars
she keeps and scatters to her liking, Mr. A
of the flawless phrasing, Madame B, who has won
many prizes, astonishing Miss C (recently up
to no good), and sweet Sir X, of whom I may have heard.

Pert, able and a born joiner, she has done well
by a ruthless study of the golden room where
everyone matters, peering through curtains to catch
the unsurpassable swirl of a skirt,
straining to hear the guests' after-dinner laughter
and dancing their measures again and again until
she knew the password and strode grandly in
while outside, bard of the usual, I haggled with the bouncer.

Now, dazzling comes so easily that she seems
always to have been there. Robust with nurture
she inhabits the room in gowns of dreamiest satin
and often, as parties reach their pitch,
can be seen enchanting kings.
Annoying exile, *I* scud into snows whose
elegant steeps and hollows I find no voice for,
sit under frail skeletons of trees
whose leafless tops show the sky at its darkest
and whose root, drowned in soil, can't touch me.

If life's a pose, no one can fairly blame her;
if, seeing me at the window late one night,
cold from the crazy paths of alien towns,
she shuts it and so forgets me (the distant tyranny
of shadows, the hot gnashing teeth of doubt),
it is ample recompense when in fragrant flavorful air,
warmed by a fire that has blazed for centuries,
she dips her pen in a lake of ink, and the pen flies.

The Late Show

And so it came about that there was no way
of crossing the river except by carrying
the special mirror, the one you found in your pocket
one winter. Orioles, crows flew over the water
and made your palms hot with lust and envy,
but to reach the other side and sit in those
ghostly deckchairs, tipsy on spiked
lemonade and insight, you need to see yourself
testing the waters. Menacing waves crashed
around a bend and broke over you;
the mirror showed a face half in love
with its own drowning. The bodies of dead dwarves came
barreling past; bales of hay were burning on the banks,
making fumes so thick that the stepping-stones
that really seemed to be getting you somewhere
showed up in the mirror as evil empires
crushing a mind that wandered where it wanted.
Saying "This way" was a way of killing those tics,
those changes of heart that made traveling fun.
When friends asked you what your trips were like,
you started pulling out the mirror and letting it
do all the talking. There on the table amid
childish inner tubes and cheap souvenirs,
it sang the praises of never getting there.

This method of fording streams having been
accepted, run with, a glossy gizmo
that loosely resembled your sturdier mirror
hit all the newsstands; travel accounts
turned cryptic and unwieldy, becoming
half-journalese, half-mandarin rambles.
A struggle became a reflex. And God only knew,
you were good at it: the stagy brow-mopping,
the true hopes of getting across, followed
by sloughs of sincerest despond, made the mirror
glint like no others. And the way fish appeared
in your glass was really magical, too:
we never knew whether you'd start describing
Jaws or a Triton. But after anyone

spends too much time with a mirror,
even its best views can start to seem
planted, not discovered. It should have
cut more, fit less easily into your hands;
sometimes when, observing your journey,
we saw a bit of river flash in your eyes,
we wanted more. We missed the time
when people like you schemed hard to start
shores bending and waves ascending. But most of all
we wondered whether you should have submitted
a little less easily to your fate:
no teleology drove you to it,
though there was, it's true, that vogue of coming
later rather than sooner. Great wader with a
hand-held mirror, what would you have done if the current
had carried it away for a day? Would the things
you saw in the rising tide have made
a duller but more intimate story?

Poem for a New Year

Love that a reign of terror struck dumb,
love that, respectful, close and clinging,
never could match the thrill of distance,
        come away from the stunted creatures;
show me your stumps and teach me why they
never grew into hands with fingers;
envy the things my feet do; tell me
        how to enjoy familiar features.

Winter that blew in like a rumor,
blew in and dragged us out of houses,
turning us into living ghosts who
        wandered around the city grieving,
win back your ruined reputation:
blanket our crimes with tender flurries,
blow back our hair and freshen it with
        patterns of ice beyond believing.

Ivy that sprouted when the cord broke,
sprouted like some old curse and soon had
people inside a haunted mansion
        walking around in savage dazes,
grow as enormous as you want to
but for the sake of comforting, not
trapping the foes who pace the carpets:
        mimic their networks, not their mazes.

Year that looms just around the corner,
looms like another chance at freedom,
study the past and know it cold, but
        feel no compulsion to repeat it:
menacing drifts of snow don't last here,
grunts of determined doubt won't work here;
when a new hand or challenge grabs me
        may I robustly, fondly meet it.

Greg Williamson

The Dark Days

I. The Cold War

We should have seen it coming back
In June: seeds of unrest, the troubled fiefdoms,
The snipers cloaked in blackjack oaks or sweetgums
    To launch an unprovoked attack

On us with mace or Minie ball,
The ministers who joked about the sage,
The sage that withered up. In our bronze age
    We missed the heralds of a fall—

The mounting shades, the Lilliputian
Insurrections waged by night—until
It dawned on us one morning with a chill,
    My God, another revolution.

The trees ran up new banners, then
In bursts of color on a bombing run
Dropped propaganda leaflets. They had won.
    "Give up," we read, "You'll never win."

In hindsight there's no mystery:
Too many palace coos, august parades,
Those slow mimosa Sundays, marmalades.
    Plus, we were young. That's history.

We should have seen it coming. Now
The slow smoke coils around the weathercocks,
All pointing north. We have set back our clocks,
    As if we could revive somehow

Our flagging, fagged esprit de corps.
The parties are over. In personal retreats
The citizens observe the empty streets
    And the dark days of the cold war.

II. S.A.D.

We should have seen it coming? Back
In June, we're told, while sweets came to the suite,
The green, spring-loaded days were packing heat,
    And, even then, insomniac

Dark forces lurked in ambuscades;
Shadows were hatching cemetery plots;
And rebel sympathizers took potshots
    With cherry bombs and rusty blades,

Till one late dawn the songbirds peeled
Away. We woke to catapulting worry:
Hannibal ad portas! With a flurry
    The world turned. Winter swept the field.

Well, that's poetic elocution,
The civil war of words, that martial art
Ascribing nature with our purple heart.
    For me, another institution.

The light died like a summer fad.
I should have seen it coming? Naturally.
The season turned, in simple terms, on me.
    I'm sated, saturated, sad.

Sometimes I change the rheostat,
But still the slow smoke coils around the clocks,
All caged in wire. We walk around in socks
    And hear dust falling in the flat

White walls we turn our faces toward.
The poems are over. In partitioned rooms
The residents observe the long, slow brooms
    And the dark daze of the cold ward.

III. Conspectus Against Anthropocentric Assumptions in
Polemical Rhetoric

We should have seen it. Coming back
In June, the sun achieved its northernmost
Ecliptic point, the solstice, which we post
Beforehand in the almanac

And on which day our region sees
The maximum of solar lumination.
Because the planet's axis of rotation
By 23.5°

Inclines from perpendicular
To the Earth's plane of orbit, seasons change
With variations in the photic range
Of our G2, main-sequence star.

Cork-celled abscission layers grow
On petioles of leaves. As chlorophyll
Dehydrates, pigments such as xanthophyll
And carotene begin to show.

Climatic shifts that coincide
With mass migrations can contribute to,
In humans, elevated rates of flu,
Fatigue, despair, and suicide.

Still, these are biological,
Not indications of occult intent.
We are a protoplasmic accident.
That is the simple truth. Let all

Of nature's signal flags be furled.
The mysteries are over. God's dead. Nor
Should one detect some latent metaphor
In the dark days of the cold world.

IV. Revised Weather Bulletin

We should have seen it coming back.
In "June" we should have heard the vestiges
of "Juno," goddess of both marriages
     And war, and seen today's snowpack

Foreshadowed in the virgin plain
Of someone's bridal gown, blizzards of rice,
The glazed and frosted wedding cake, and ice-
     Bound, listing bottles of champagne,

Portending future dissolution.
We should have seen it coming back because,
While seasons change with scientific laws,
     cf., another attribution:

"All things are metaphors," the Sage
Of Weimar said. And I have evidence,
The inside dope, counterintelligence:
     Flybys of geese, the heavy-gauge

Entanglements of trees, the charge
Of winter storm troops, and the clicking Morse
Of sleet detail the occupation force
     Of nature, standing by and large

For warfare, silencings, and fear.
Now long shades muster in the empty streets,
All choked in ice. The light brigade retreats
     To foothills of the last frontier,

And gray coats move in undeterred.
The year is over. In the studio
I see the long-range forecast calls for snow
     And the dark days of the cold word.

Bodies of Water

Glimmerings are what the soul's composed of.
　　　　　　　　　　　　　　　—Seamus Heaney

Yes, but the body is made of water. That's
　　　　A fact. It freezes with its fear
And boils with rage because it has states.
　　　　It blows off steam. It swells with pride.
　　　　　　　　It sweats like a pipe,
　　　　　　　　But it is water.

Genetic pool, swamp of desires, its heart
　　　　　　　　Melts at a beautiful face;
Turned to a puddle, it stands in the street and admires.
　　　　The body runs hot and cold and down
　　　　　　　　In soaked beds,
　　　　　　　　Seeking its level.

There have been souls who drowned in pity, drowned
　　　　　　　　In sorrow. Just last week,
There was a glimmer of something out on the surface,
　　　　Then it went under. When divers went in
　　　　　　　　They found gold teeth
　　　　　　　　And hundreds of miles of water.

Appalachian Trees Encircled by Police Tape

—from *Double Exposures*

　　　　　　　　Conveying the effects of atmosphere,
Yellow police tape bounds a tranquil place.
　　　　　　　　It's my *plein air* Impressionist landscape. Here
It's a crime scene, another open case.
　　　　　　　　The trees are being poisoned, dying, like Swift,
But the authorities refuse to talk
　　　　　　　　From the top down. Wordsworthian breezes drift
About it all. An outline's drawn in chalk;

From heartland and high hills to the town square,
They're checking for prints. We know the scene by heart,
                But something's in the air, in the plain air.
(Where inspiration's said to come for art.)

Belvedere Marittimo

My dear, you would not believe the weather here.
The postcard doesn't do it justice, nor
Can I. But notice how the sun's great mint
Is stamping silver coins upon the sea,
Scooning away whole treasuries of change
On pelicans, bikinis, the lacy flounce
Of surf. And notice, too, in the flowerbed
How lady-slippers and narcissi blush
Beside the bedsheets luffing on a line
And how the watercolor limes and pinks
Of the little summer cottages appear
To be the very picture of repose.

For seven days I've looked out of my room
On none of this. A bankrupt, dishrag sky
Wrings out a steady mizzle on the beach,
An indigent hachure which drains away
The washes of pastel to shades of gray
As bleary, wet, and untranslatable
As every sodden page of *il giornale*.
Sinister, small black birds clothespin the line.
"The piers are pummelled by the waves." I write,
Perhaps, to weather this foul weather, dear.
The rain runs down the glass. Wish you were here.

Max Winter

Elegy

There is a question
at the bottom of every potter's field.
It wears long pants and suspenders
and pours you a drink
as it leans away from the sun.
I was walking south through the city
on a Sunday afternoon
and I saw the question
scuttling in the shadows.
I confronted it with my palm open
and the voice of a little angel
and was left with nothing but tears.
The city filled with wind and dust.
We blew into the ocean.
I soon became a cloud
hiding the kingfisher that flies through our dreams
to keep us honest.

Space Parable

I had pelted the robot with all
manner of missiles but still
it would not give up the information.

Back in the pod,
I was held responsible
for the ultimate destruction of everything.

Even Professor Marienbad,
humbled as he was by invisible meteors,
would not receive me in his study.

I wiped the astral windshield,
scrubbed the neutron pots,
scoured the spoons with stardust.

My Airedale mug was broken while I slept.
My go-cart racing trophy lost its polish.
My letters never reached the planet Earth.

And then, for good behavior, I received
another walk on the fiery surface.
I thrilled at the chance—but went blank at the thought.

When I came to, I saw the robot
standing above me, shaking his head
with gravity, extending his map.

Like a punishment. Like my name was Rex,
or something. I grumbled to the easternmost crater.
I scribbled with a stick among the radioactive particles.

And they never heard from me again.
The ship went dim.
A world exploded its petals into space.

Long Distance

These songs in my ears are enough
to make a flash-lit city fall in love.
I should be sleeping.
I would pay cold cash to be
what is called "human" for short.
Transistors coughing, everywhere.
The ash trees have asked me to be more clear.
I have run out of air to swallow
and I cannot possibly last
until morning opens its toolbox.
I will wait for you
in the wide between a pair of tributaries.

From here I can see the engineer quite clearly.
Perhaps I will find my desire in Axle Falls, Ohio,
under a glowing Vacancy.
Have I told you lately that I love to close my eyes?
Something jams underneath us,
possibly something irreplaceable,
and then the man who lives inside my ache
leads me through a map of the territory.
(I am just a hillock, hurting no one.)
And then he calls the number
marked between my ribs
to say to me I lose my touch
with each mile away from Allegheny, Pennsylvania.
Tell me
this is not what it means to be human.

Dux Bellorum

The shirt I sleep in
has two words printed on it:
"tundra" on the front,
"Gethsemane" on the back.
The person who painted those words
watches me at night from my rocking chair
while I sleep half-covered by blankets.
He appears at the edge of my dreams,
swinging a lantern fueled by the concentration
it takes to create a life like mine.

The shirt I sleep in
is moth-eaten, I say
when people ask me how I'm doing,
how I spend my waking hours.
Depending on my mood,
I might also make a shadow-box
in the pure afternoon air.
Invitations come seldom.
I prefer to eat my haute cuisine

on the frozen side of town,
buying my ostensible subject,
always late with cold red cheeks,
a bottomless cup of coffee.

The shirt I sleep in
has a thousand wrongs to confess.
I try to calm it with hand claps
or one-line incantations,
but there is no lasting cure.
Once, in the dead of spring,
when everyone I knew lived
close enough to happiness to snatch it
in the blink of a passing train,
my shirt spoke so loudly for so long
that finally I tossed it in my closet.
It didn't learn to shut its mouth,
and to this day I sell alarm clocks
on a boulevard of sentences broken
from line to line to line.

Sam Witt

Michael Masse

Blue thigh of daybreak, sweetened, fall apart—
my fourteenth year: a drop of oil on his thigh.
I know that room like the back of my heart,
aquarium blue: subcutaneous: a lambent sigh . . .

September: sleeve of drowsy hornets: the fallen pear glutted with blood:
I did not warm myself over that heat.

One man's soft spot is another man's temple.
fifteen, sixteen, I'm silver-tongued—"Ssshhh . . . they'll hear."
And swallowing his white hair in headlight, simple,
one man's juiced footprints are my rotting pear.

Gallowgrass, nodding off outside in the wind—Michael, I said—
face of wept meat—

A taper, dripping tallow on my gut.
A swallow's feather curling into smoke,
and breath—for we are the very food of light—
a fingery gaze, a breeze that scalds the lake.

And your flesh? The tiny bloodrose where his lips withdrew.
And your kiss?

A dolphin's back that lifts me in a dive:
I fall into that softening and live.

Waterfowl Descending

Shall speak to me in their fattening echo, & purr: penetralia,
& the moaning—

The meadow darkens quietly: "the sleep of reason."
My weights: a transponder that looms, spindle & truss, all that I was

flashing once from the standing water, & white.

In the tall grass I have an exceptionally long neck, blueish
& metallic in its sheen.

The one brushing a surface with his broken wing, without wings.
The one unable to ask.

In the grasses I flick my eyes open like an iguana about to suckle . . .

Suckles my injured, reflected hair when I kneel in the water.
Desiccates me cold, a pygmy ravishing an orange.

For those of us who have sinned, pray for us,
I am bathed in a thinner sky, pray for me, each soft,

empty landing a report of my dying now, a backbeat.

(Report: the wind manages to get through me)

Unfathered, unencrypted through the air, gasoline transpiring.
For those of us who breathe, but your ear

splendidly & cheaply to the ground as they fluster,
imitation parrotmeat, & a bronze feather that falls: my cheeks

flushed, "like the sky at dawn,"

when tall colors reach heavenward, & sicken,
& die-

          Once, I drew a picture
of fowl abreast a hillside, a simple injury, I was a little girl

laughing in the dark, my sylph. These

swift, flicking motions—precisely now—they are beading me
with her small eyes,

& the air sparkles with prerecorded applause,
a delicate weft into the sky, unspooling & saccadic. An

orphan bird, (a cylinder) of many
colourful sounds I could not decipher, its slick feathers

as of spunne glass to a red throat,

(revolving in my chest when soft thermides die—)

shall sicken just back of the ear (& dyed): I heard
what voices we must have been, hlanc, & slender,

hugging the ground when they traveled: hunger,

I am worth my weight in horsemeat.

(Debride: "only the wind shall light your hair on fire,")

onely the grass get through me
who have preyen.

(—aftermath: a second growth of grass in a season—)

They were coming down to visit me when the air parts,
They were lacerating my throte & hungry

(when soft voices die)

into dozens of wishing wings.

Americana

Onely in thy wig, Sister, does the sky clear—

hush of a June shower, lashed flesh of a sapling that bleeds the sky

to the color of bathwater, a thin dish of sunset
for tall colors, like *us*, to sip.

On Tuesdays, like today, I can only perform simple tasks.
Listening to squirrels build a lovely nest between the walls,

the human scamper of those tiny, whispering feet.

Pulling dark, Sister, the powdered hair over my poor,
my broken crown on the front stoop,

I have an earwig that sings, *speak, Sister, that I may know thee* . . .

As station wagons pass me by, I am too lazy to eat,
blue-eyd & forgotten,

fingering the oversized, marshmallow peanuts from certain truckstops,
a coward to my own bald thoughts.

On Tuesday I swallowed a monstrous mouthful of bathwater,
& forgot.

Forgot my slender hair washing in the wind.

For nine long years behind smokd glass I slept, my throte
of silver embalmd,

nine long months enwrappd in your fleckd voice, Sister, singing: *sleep,*

("sleep in a grainfield on your feet, & the sweep of the grain

shall be a great river overspilling its banks, a woman, brother, you & I,
letting our long hair down,

speaking in many soft fingers to the wind—") Lethe-sister,
I have my life to drink.

I do not belong here, I belong everywhere, a tiny speechless
pinwheel of sparks

that hanged in the sky, unchanged & changing, of acetylene
that cries so brightly in the sun:

("You must not speak of the long hairs that sufferd through us—")
Its long, tired tail of frozen gas

dragged across the sky (& blue,) nodding off into our long wake,
savage & lean, Sister, in my hungry cry,

a human hair borne through the blue, a hairbell, playd out in the wind.

I *am* the miracle fabric, that flash
when you flipped your hair in the sunshine ages ago,

(onely you know it's a wig) & fade fast, (it's my life,) shorne away,
stroked by tired fingers now on my knees,

(You must not pet the wigs when I smell candle wax on an empty stair)
thy empty face, hung with starres now, & frozen dewe,

On the First and Last Day, Sister,
(O weave me a shirt of that black, black hair that I may live)

when I spilled from myself & away.

Everlasting Quail

Then the air was a brutal architecture of sugar.

Boys wading to their knees
into blue carpeting,

centurions at dawn, waist-deep in the street
& drunk, looking for her-

Meanwhile the cherry tree was dripping with bees,
a tremble of everlasting quail . . .

I left my wife in a tall hotel.

Wasn't that the room where they grew bigger trees?
There were tall buildings darkening in the clouds.

(Human: I must have been an enormous bishop
swinging a silver teaball in the kitchen.)

And today, a day so peaceful & sunny-side up,
a day for being alive.

The day I am scheduled to lose my mouth?
Everybody has spoken through this throat:

"I don't think in the end God wishes us to be human"
where money lies down on the floor.

She was a smudged photo of sleep, her blonde
empty cheeks faceless & streaming.

I dropped a coin into her mouth
and walked off.

(At night I repeat the word "pillow."

Pillow: a naked footstep slapping the pavement.
Orphan: the wind that eats my laughing chest,)

empty: my laughing chest: my cheeks.

Mark Wunderlich

The Bruise of This

The night I woke to find the sheets wet from you,
like a man cast up on the beach,
I hurried you off to the shower to cool you down,

dressed you, the garments strict and awkward in my hands,
and got you into a taxi to the hospital,
the driver eyeing us from his rearview mirror—

The blue tone of the paging bell,
the green smocks, metal beds,
plastic chairs linked

in a childhood diagram of infection,
and when they wheeled you by
there was a needle in your arm,

the bruise of this
already showing itself,
and rather than watch gloved doctors handle you

in their startling white coats and loose ties,
I took a seat outside and waited,
time yawning, thick and static—

and made clear to me in the bright light of speculation
was time's obstacle in the body,
and those things I could do that might cushion it.

From a Vacant House

It is hard to want a thing you know will hurt another,
yet the heart persists, doesn't it, with its dark urges, liquid wish?

A sea town. Gulls, those malefica, uselessly scissor
thin-boned bodies against a beach washed of its will,

where a season ago women lay, dogs and children fastened
to the long arms of their concern, the men vacant and glittery

with spandex and oil. It is November, and already the books thicken
at my bedside, a crush of paper characters awaiting the eye's

hurried pass, their unread stories attendant through the night,
until its bandage lifts to a morning blush, and I am held

with the parenthesis of a spare white house, a little thinner,
empty hands chilled like the faithful, offering myself to discipline's

cool machinery. I will stand on the pier, gesturing and cold.
I will open my mouth to your opening mouth.

Take Good Care of Yourself

On the runway at the Roxy, the drag queen
fans herself gently, but with purpose.
She is an Asian princess, an elaborate wig
jangling like bells on a Shinto temple,
shoulders broad as my father's. With a flick

of her fan she covers her face, a whole
world of authority in that one gesture,
a screen sliding back, all black lacquer
and soprano laugh. The music in this place
echoes with the whip-crack of 2,000

men's libidos, and the one bitter pill
of X-tasy dissolving on my tongue is the perfect
slender measure of the holy ghost,
the vibe crawling my spine exactly,
I assure myself, what I've always wanted.

It is 1992. There is no *you* yet for me
to address, just simple imperative. *Give*
me more. Give. It is a vision, I'm sure
of this, of what heaven might provide—a sea
of men all muscle, white briefs and pearls,

of kilts cut too short for Catholic girls
or a Highland fling. Don't bother with chat
just yet. I've stripped and checked my shirt
at the door. I need a drink, a light, someplace
a little cooler, just for a minute, to chill.

There is no place like the unbearable ribbon
of highway that cuts the Midwest into two unequal
halves, a pale sun glowing like the fire
of one last cigarette. It is the prairie
I'm scared of, barreling off in all directions

flat as its inhabitants A's and O's. I left
Wisconsin's well-tempered rooms
and snow-fields white and vacant as a bed
I wish I'd never slept in. Winters
I stared out the bus window through frost

at an icy template of what the world offered up—
the moon's tin cup of romance and a beauty,
that if held too long to the body,
would melt. If I'd felt anything for you then
it was mere, the flicker of possibility

a quickening of the pulse when I imagined
a future, not here but elsewhere, the sky
not yawning out, but hemmed in. In her dress
the drag is all glitter and perfect grace,
pure artifice, beating her fan, injuring

the smoky air, and in the club, I'm still
imagining. The stacks of speakers burn
and throb, whole cities of sound bear down
on us. I'm dancing with men all around me,
moving every muscle I can, the woman's voice

mixed and extended to a gorgeous black note
in a song that only now can I remember—
one familiar flat stretch, one wide-open vista
and a rhythm married to words
for what we still had to lose.

The Anchorage

I think you would like this seaside town—it makes me dream of whales.
All night they break through the dark, unhinging monstrous jaws,

their flukes stirring the surface to an oily calm
while gulls swoop to pull the krill from the great open maw

and all day I've been thinking of the twelfth-century postulant
sealed as a child in the monastery wall, sealed with her anchor.

Together the women sang the canticles, opening
only for the priest's bony finger touching the sacrament

to their lips, then the sour sponge of Christ's blood, kissed
back. Years ago, I walked an overgrown road through the woods

where bees turned treble arcs in a haze of goldenrod
and rusting hulks of implements leached red on the ground.

There the white came in. It came in to flood my brain,
and if I did not know it was vascular, I'd swear

it was some facsimile of heaven—seven platinum spheres rotating
over shifting tiles, then a veil hemmed in ten thousand stitches

of light, the pain a toll for foresight's privilege.
And in the migraine's aftermath, the glass lid lifted up,

the doves whistling plaintive as ghosts, this is when
flesh married suffering in the mind. Above my bed

I still have the picture of the Virgin Mary—tender feet
braced on a crescent moon's gold hooks, a cape

spilling with roses, desert-rare and pungent
as the flowering vines crawling my own house's window,

where I would sit sealed behind the shut lids of the blinds,
hidden from a cold-shocked sky, thinking how a body satisfies.

I've moved six times since then, farther from that northern lake's
glass eye, with its cataracts of fish shacks,

the tar-paper house where laundry webbed the shrubs,
cats coiled in window wells, the mop water

freezing on the floors and my breath clouding as I crept
the stairs to my room. Here at the shore, I still live

with the threat of seizure, but fear it not as much,
heaven less my childhood vision of a bleached and rotating city

than a rocking and viscous zone of slow-moving figures,
our shadows sealed together, opening for the holiest sustenance.

There will be no blood there, no virus linking up its cellular chains
to consume the flesh, no houses remembered for the shapes

that move through them. Just motion, and union, and light.

Kevin Young

Quivira City Limits

for Thomas Fox Averill

Pull over. Your car with its slow
breathing. Somewhere outside Topeka

it suddenly all matters again,
those tractors blooming rust

in the fields only need a good coat
of paint. Red. You had to see

for yourself, didn't you; see that the world
never turned small, transportation

just got better; to learn
we can't say a town or a baseball

team without breathing in
a dead Indian. To discover why Coronado

pushed up here, following the guide
who said he knew fields of gold,

north, who led them past these plains,
past buffaloes dark as he was. Look.

Nothing but the wheat, waving them
sick, a sea. While they strangle

him blue as the sky above you
The Moor must also wonder

when will all this ever be enough?
this wide open they call discovery,

disappointment, this place my
thousand bones carry, now call home.

Clyde Peeling's Reptiland in Allenwood, Pennsylvania

You must admit it's natural
that while waiting for the three o'clock
informational reptile handling & petting

show, we all imagined a few choice tragedies,
maybe a snake devouring one of the six
identical blond children in the front row,

or the anaconda choking on all five
badly braided girls. I confess openly
we discussed ways in which the obnoxious

crying child in the third row actually wriggled
free of daddy's constricting arms, his head opened
against the ground like a melon & a ripe one

at that. See, in the end the tragedy is all
in the telling, not at the moment when the gator
slips out of Ched Peeling's trusty, thoroughbred

hands & gobbles down a few select
youngsters—preferably the really loud or
beautiful ones—but later, after the ambulances

have sped away & no one breathes
a word. Even when everything is said
& done, I don't know whether only the loud

& really beautiful things get remembered
or most things just grow loud & beautiful
when gone. I can only tell you

that later I thought for hours about Irvy
the Alligator's smooth underbelly & the way
it drove him nearly extinct, how folks once

looked at him & called him desire, a handbag
in waiting. How you won't drive past any Negrolands
on your way through Pennsylvania, or anywhere

else in this union. How while learning about lizards
that grow their tails back, bloodless, I kept
thinking The Colored Zoo may be exactly what

we need, a pleasant place to find out how They eat
watermelon & mate regularly, a cool comfortable
room where everyone can sit around

& ask *How do I recognize*
one or protect myself? or *Their hair,*
how do They get it to clench up

like that? A guide dressed in unthreatening
greens or a color we don't have to call
brown could reply *Good question,*

then hold one up & demonstrate, show
all the key markings. But you must
believe me when I say there is not really

such a place, when I tell you that I held
my breath with the rest at Reptiland, listening
to Ched recite his snakebite story for the four-

hundredth time, waving around his middle finger
where the rattler sunk fangs. You must forgive
how we leaned closer as he described venom

eating green & cold through his veins, pictured
perfectly its slow nauseous seep, like watching
the eleven o'clock footage of someone beaten

blue by the cops, over & over, knowing you could
do nothing about this, only watch, knowing
it already has all happened without you

& probably will keep on happening, steady
as snake poison traveling toward the heart,
the way these things go on by, slowly,

an ancient turtle we pay
to pet as it walks past,
souvenir, survivor.

Letters from the North Star

Dear you: the lights here ask
nothing, the white falling
around my letters silent,
unstoppable. I am writing this
from the empty stomach of sleep

where nothing but the cold
wonders where you're headed;
nobody here peels heads sour
and cheap as lemon, and only
the car sings AM the whole

night through. In the city,
I have seen children half-
bitten by wind. Even trains
arrive without a soul
to greet them; things do

not need me here, this world
dances on its own. Only bridges
beg for me to make them
famous, to learn what I had
almost forgotten of flying,

of soaring free, south,
down. So long. Xs, Os.

Campbell's Black Bean Soup

Candid, Warhol
scoffed, coined it
a nigger's loft—

not The Factory,
Basquiat's studio stood
anything but lofty—

skid rows of canvases,
paint peeling like bananas,
scabs. Bartering work

for horse, Basquiat churned
out butter, signing each
SAMO©. Sameold. Sambo's

soup. How to sell out
something bankrupt
already? How to copy

rights? Basquiat stripped
labels, opened & ate
alphabets, chicken

& noodle. Not even brown
broth left beneath, not one
black bean, he smacked

the very bottom, scraping
the uncanny, making
a tin thing sing.

Langston Hughes

LANGSTON HUGHES
LANGSTON HUGHES
  O come now
  & sang
them weary blues—

Been tired here
feelin' low down
  Real
  tired here
since you quit town

Our ears no longer trumpets
Our mouths no more bells
  FAMOUS POET©—
  Busboy—Do tell
us of hell—

Mr. Shakespeare in Harlem
Mr. Theme for English B
  Preach on
  kind sir
of death, if it please—

We got no more promise
We only got ain't
  Let us in
  on how
you 'came a saint

LANGSTON
LANGSTON
  LANGSTON HUGHES
  Won't you send
all heaven's news

Acknowledgments

: : : : :

Contributors

Acknowledgments

Sherman Alexie: "Theology" first appeared in *Prairie Schooner*, © 1997 Sherman Alexie. "The Exaggeration of Despair" is reprinted from *The Summer of Black Widows* © 1996 Sherman Alexie, by permission of Hanging Loose Press. "Evolution" is reprinted from *The Business of Fancydancing*, © 1992 Sherman Alexie, by permission of Hanging Loose Press. "I Would Steal Horses" is reprinted from *First Indian on the Moon*, © 1993 Sherman Alexie, by permission of Hanging Loose Press.

Talvikki Ansel: "You Don't Know What Happened When You Froze" and "My Shining Archipelago" are reprinted from *My Shining Archipelago* by Talvikki Ansel by permission of Yale University Press and the author. © 1997 Talvikki Ansel. "For Want" and "Origin Charm Against Uncertain Injuries" appear courtesy of the author, © 1999 Talvikki Ansel.

Rick Barot: "Three Amoretti" first appeared in *New England Review*, © 1998 Rick Barot. "Portishead Suite" first appeared in *Colorado Review*, © 1999 Rick Barot. "Riffing" first appeared in the *Georgia Review*, © 1998 Rick Barot.

Paul Beatty: "That's Not in My Job Description" is reprinted from *Joker, Joker, Deuce* by Paul Beatty, © 1994 Paul Beatty. Used by permission of Viking Penguin, a division of Penguin Putnam Inc.

Erin Belieu: "A Sleeping Man Must Be Awakened to Be Killed," "Rondeau at the Train Stop," and "Legend of the Albino Farm" from *Infanta*, © 1995; "Nocturne: My Sister Life" from *Brown Recluse*, © 1999 Erin Belieu. Reprinted by permission of Copper Canyon Press, Post Office Box 271, Port Townsend, WA 98368.

Rafael Campo: "The Battle Hymn of the Republic," "My Childhood in Another Part of the World," "Asylum," and "What the Body Told" are reprinted from *What the Body Told* by Rafael Campo, © 1996 Duke University Press. All rights reserved. Used with permission. "Towards Curing AIDS" is reprinted with permission from the publisher of *The Other Man Was Me: A Voyage to the New World* (Houston: Arte Público Press-University of Houston, 1994), © 1994 Arte Público Press.

Nick Carbó: "When the grain is golden and . . . ," "Little Brown Brother," "The Filipino Politician," and "Votive Candles" are reprinted from *El Gruppo McDonalds* by Nick Carbó by permission of Tia Chucha Press and the author, © 1995 Nick Carbó.

Joshua Clover: "The Map Room" and "*El Periférico, or Sleep*" are reprinted by permission of Louisiana State University Press from *Madonna anno domini: Poems*, by Joshua Clover. Copyright © 1997 Joshua Clover. "An archive of confessions, a genealogy of confessions" and "Alas, that is the name of our town; I have been concealing it all this time" both appear courtesy of the author, © 1999 Joshua Clover.

Nicole Cooley: "The Mother: Dorcas Good," and "Publick Fast on Account of the Afflicted: March 31, 1692" all appear courtesy of the author, © 1999 Nicole Cooley. "Mary Warren's Sampler" first appeared in *New England Review*, © 1999 Nicole Cooley. "John Winthrop . . ." first appeared in the *Missouri Review*, © 1999 Nicole Cooley.

Denise Duhamel: "How Much Is This Poem Going to Cost Me?", "I'm Dealing with My Pain," and "Sex with a Famous Poet" are reprinted from *The Star-Spangled Banner* by Denise Duhamel, © 1999 Southern Illinois University Press. "Ego" first appeared in *Prairie Schooner*, © 1999 Denise Duhamel.

Thomas Sayers Ellis: "Star Child" first appeared in *AGNI*, © 1995 Thomas Sayers Ellis. "Atomic Bride" first appeared in *Ploughshares*, © 1996 Thomas Sayers Ellis. "Sir Nose D'VoidofFunk" first appeared in *Callaloo*, © 1998 Thomas Sayers Ellis. "Practice" first appeared in the *Boston Book Review*, © 1999 Thomas Sayers Ellis.

Suzanne Gardinier: "Democracy" (Nothing hurts but the foot is insistent), "The Ghost of Santo Domingo" (I've set six stones in a row near the eastern), and "Admirals (Columbus)" (The people go naked men and women) from *The New World* by Suzanne Gardinier, © 1993. Reprinted by permission of the University of Pittsburgh Press. "Letter to My Mother" first appeared in *Under 35: The New Generation of American Poets* (Doubleday, 1989), © 1989 Suzanne Gardinier. "Two Girls" first appeared in the *American Voice*, © 1995 Suzanne Gardinier.

James Harms: "My Androgynous Years" is reprinted from *Modern Ocean* by permission of Carnegie Mellon University Press and the author, © 1992 James Harms. "The Joy Addict," "Soon," and "Los Angeles, the Angels" are reprinted from *The Joy Addict* by permission of Carnegie Mellon University Press and the author, © 1998

James Harms. "Soon" first appeared in the *Kenyon Review,* © 1997 James Harms. "Los Angeles, the Angels," first appeared in *Poetry Northwest,* © 1997 James Harms.

Allison Joseph: "Numbers" and "Pure Pop" first appeared in *Prairie Schooner.* © 1997 Allison Joseph. "My Father's Heroes" from *In Every Seam,* by Allison Joseph, © 1997. Reprinted by permission of the University of Pittsburgh Press.

Julia Kasdorf: "Green Market, New York," "When Our Women Go Crazy," "Grossdaadi's Funeral," and "Mennonites" from *Sleeping Preacher,* by Julia Kasdorf, © 1992. Reprinted by permission of the University of Pittsburgh Press. "Eve's Striptease" from *Eve's Striptease,* by Julia Kasdorf, © 1998. Reprinted by permission of the University of Pittsburgh Press.

Joy Katz: "The Imperfect Is Our Paradise" first appeared in *Quarterly West,* © 1998 Joy Katz. "Taxonomy" first appeared in *Parnassus: Poetry in Review,* © 1996 Joy Katz. "Concerning the Islands Newly Discovered" first appeared in the *Fiddlehead,* © 1995 Joy Katz. "Women Must Put Off Their Rich Apparel," first appeared in *Pleiades,* © 1997 Joy Katz. "Falling" first appeared in *Antioch Review,* © 1996 Joy Katz.

Timothy Liu: "Ariel Singing" and "Vox Angelica" from *Vox Angelica* by Timothy Liu by permission of Alice James Books, 1992. "Kindertotenlieder" and "Poem" from *Say Goodnight,* © 1998; "Sunday" from *Burnt Offerings,* © 1995 Timothy Liu. Reprinted by permission of Copper Canyon Press, Post Office Box 271, Port Townsend, WA 98368.

Khaled Mattawa: "Watermelon Tales" is reprinted from *Ismailia Eclipse* by Khaled Mattawa by permission of Sheep Meadow Press and the author, © 1995 Khaled Mattawa. "Heartsong" first appeared in *Ploughshares,* © 1996 Khaled Mattawa. "Before" appears courtesy of the author, © 1999 Khaled Mattawa.

Jeffrey McDaniel: "Disasterology," "D," and "Following Her to Sleep" are reprinted from *Alibi School* by Jeffrey McDaniel by permission of Manic D Press and the author, © 1995 Jeffrey McDaniel. "Logic in the House of Sawed-Off Telescopes" is reprinted from *The Forgiveness Parade* by Jeffrey McDaniel by permission of Manic D Press and the author, © 1998 Manic D Press.

Campbell McGrath: "The First Trimester," "Delphos, Ohio," and "Spring Comes to Chicago" from *Spring Comes to Chicago* by Campbell McGrath. Copyright © 1996 Campbell McGrath. Reprinted by permission of The Ecco Press. "Wheatfield Under Clouded Sky" from *American Noise* by Campbell

McGrath. Copyright © 1993 Campbell McGrath. Reprinted by permission of The Ecco Press.

HeidiLynn Nilsson: "'We Are Easily Reduced'" first appeared in *TriQuarterly*, © 1997 HeidiLynn Nilsson. "My Least Skirtable Deficiency" first appeared in *Pleiades*, © 1998 HeidiLynn Nilsson. "How Came What Came Alas" first appeared in *Pleiades*, © 1999 HeidiLynn Nilsson. "On Inheriting Departure" is printed by permission of the author, © 1997 HeidiLynn Nilsson.

Rick Noguchi: "The Turn of Privacy," "The Breath He Holds," "I, the Neighbor Mr. Uskovich, Watch Every Morning Kenji Takezo Hold His Breath," "The Really Long Ride," "From Rooftops, Kenji Takezo Throws Himself," and "Kenji Takezo Becomes Water" from *The Ocean Inside Kenji Takezo*, by Rick Noguchi, © 1996. Reprinted by permission of the University of Pittsburgh Press.

Barbara J. Orton: "Love Poem" and "Beekeeper" first appeared in the *Literary Review*, © 1995 and © 1998 Barbara J. Orton. "The Sea Monkeys" first appeared in *Verse*, © 1998 Barbara J. Orton. "Bacchanal" first appeared in the *Laurel Review*, © 1996 Barbara J. Orton.

Alan Michael Parker: "The Vandals," "Another Poem about the Vandals," and "Cruelty, the Vandals Say," copyright © 1999 Alan Michael Parker. Reprinted from *The Vandals* with the permission of BOA Editions, Ltd., 260 East Ave., Rochester, NY 14604. "Days like Prose" © 1997 Alan Michael Parker. Reprinted from *Days like Prose* by permission of Alef Books. "No Fool, the God of Salt" and "The God of Pepper" first appeared in *Triquarterly*, © 1999 Alan Michael Parker.

D. A. Powell: "[nicholas the ridiculous: you will always be 27 and impossible. no more expectations]," "[the thickness of victor decreased: blanket->sheet->floss. until no material would do]," "[sleek mechanical dart: the syringe noses into the blue vein marking the target of me]," "[who won't praise green. each minute to caress each minute blade of spring. green slice us open]" from *Tea*, © 1998 D. A. Powell, Wesleyan University Press, reprinted by permission of University Press of New England. "[sonnet]" first appeared in *Pleiades*. © 1999 D. A. Powell. "[darling can you kill me: with your mickeymouse pillows]" first appeared in *Pequod*. © 1999 D. A. Powell.

Claudia Rankine: "Testimonial" is reprinted from *The End of the Alphabet* by Claudia Rankine by permission of Grove Press and the author, © 1998 Claudia Rankine.

Matthew Rohrer: "Precision German Craftsmanship" first appeared in *Chicago Review*, © 1999 Matthew Rohrer. "Brooklyn Bridge" and "Gliding Toward the Lamps" appear courtesy of the author, © 1999 Matthew Rohrer. "The Hunger of the Lemur" first appeared in *Boston Review*, © 1998 Matthew Rohrer.

Ruth L. Schwartz: "Why I Forgive My Younger Self Her Transgressions" first appeared in *Chelsea*, © 1994 Ruth L. Schwartz. "Midnight Supper" first appeared in *My Lover Is a Woman: Contemporary Lesbian Love Poems* edited by L. Newman (Ballantine Books, 1996), © 1996 Ruth L. Schwartz. "Falling in Love after Forty" appears courtesy of the author, © 1999 Ruth L. Schwartz. "AIDS Education, Seventh Grade" from *Accordian Breathing and Dancing*, by Ruth L. Schwartz, © 1995. Reprinted by permission of the University of Pittsburgh Press.

Angela Shaw: "Crepuscule" first appeared in *Poetry*, © 1995 The Modern Poetry Association. Reprinted by permission of the editor of *Poetry*. "Rear Window" first appeared in *Field*, © 1997 Angela Shaw, "April" first appeared in *Chelsea*, © 1993 Angela Shaw. "Small Pleasures" first appeared in *Indiana Review*, © 1995 Angela Shaw. "Bird Nests" first appeared in *Seneca Review*, © 1997 Angela Shaw.

Reginald Shepherd: "The Difficult Music" from *Some are Drowning*, by Reginald Shepherd. © 1994. Reprinted by permission of the University of Pittsburgh Press. "Another Version of an Ocean" and "The Gods at Three A.M." from *Angel, Interrupted*, by Reginald Shepherd, © 1996. Reprinted by permission of the University of Pittsburgh Press. "Motive" from *Wrong*, by Reginald Shepherd, © 1999. Reprinted by permission of the University of Pittsburgh Press.

Larissa Szporluk: "Holy Ghost," "Occupant of the House," and "Axiom of Maria" from *Dark Sky Question* by Larissa Szporluk, © 1998 Larissa Szporluk. Reprinted by permission of Beacon Press, Boston. "Triage" first appeared in *Pleiades*, © 2000 Larissa Szporluk.

Ann Townsend: "Mardi Gras Premortem," "First Death," "The Bicycle Racers," "Purple Loosestrife," and "Rouge" are reprinted from *Dime Store Erotics* by permission of Silverfish Review Press and the author, © 1998 Ann Townsend.

Natasha Trethewey: "Naola Beauty Academy: New Orleans, Louisiana 1943" first appeared in *AGNI*, © 1993 Natasha Trethewey. "Bellocq's Ophelia" first appeared in the *Southern Review*, © 1998 Natasha Trethewey. "Cameo" first appeared in *Crazyhorse*, © 1999 Natasha Trethewey. "Photograph of a Bawd Drinking Raleigh Rye" appears courtesy of the author, © 1999 Natasha Trethewey.

Karen Volkman: "Daffodils" and "Shipwreck Poem" from *Crash's Law* by Karen Volkman. Copyright © 1996 Karen Volkman. Reprinted by permission of W. W. Norton & Company, Inc. "Shrewd star, who crudes . . ." first appeared in *Chelsea,* © 1998 Karen Volkman. "I won't go in today . . ." first appeared in *Colorado Review,* © 1996 Karen Volkman. "We did things more dulcet . . ." first appeared in *Boston Review,* © 1998 Karen Volkman.

Rachel Wetzsteon: "Urban Gallery" and "Drinks in the Town Square" from *The Other Stars* by Rachel Wetzsteon. Copyright © 1994 Rachel Wetzsteon. Used by permission of Penguin, a division of Penguin Putnam Inc. "Poem for a New Year," "A Rival," and "The Late Show" from *Home and Away* by Rachel Wetzsteon. Copyright © 1998 Rachel Wetzsteon. Used by permission of Penguin, a division of Viking Penguin Putnam Inc.

Greg Williamson: "The Dark Days" first appeared in the *Yale Review,* © 1997 Greg Williamson. "Bodies of Water" first appeared in *New England Review,* © 1998 Greg Williamson. "Appalachian Trees Encircled by Police Tape" appears courtesy of the author, © 1999 Greg Williamson. "Belvedere Marittimo" is reprinted from *The Silent Partner* by permission of Story Line Press and the author, © 1995 Greg Williamson.

Max Winter: "Space Parable," "Dux Bellorum," and "Long Distance" appear courtesy of the author, © 1999 Max Winter. "Elegy" first appeared in *Boulevard,* © 1997 Max Winter.

Sam Witt: "Americana," "Everlasting Quail," "Waterfowl Descending," and "Michael Masse" appear courtesy of the author, © 1998 Sam Witt.

Mark Wunderlich: "The Bruise of This," "From a Vacant House," "Take Good Care of Yourself," and "The Anchorage" are reprinted from *The Anchorage* by permission of University of Massachusetts Press, © 1999 the University of Massachusetts Press.

Kevin Young: Three poems, "Quivira City Limits," "Clyde Peeling's Reptiland in Allenwood, Pennsylvania," and "Letters from the North Star," are reprinted from *Most Way Home* by Kevin Young. Copyright © 1995 Kevin Young/Fisted Pick Productions. By permission of William Morrow Company, Inc. "Campbell's Black Bean Soup" first appeared in *Hambone,* © 1997 Kevin Young. "Langston Hughes" first appeared in the *New Yorker,* © 1999 Kevin Young.

Contributors

Sherman Alexie was born in Spokane, Washington, in 1966 and grew up in Wellpinit, Washington, on the Spokane Indian Reservation. A Spokane/Coeur d'Alene Indian, he attended Gonzaga University and received his BA in American studies from Washington State University. He now lives in Seattle, Washington, with his wife and son.

Alexie has published twelve books of fiction and poetry, including *Indian Killer, The Business of Fancydancing, The Lone Ranger and Tonto Fistfight in Heaven, The Summer of Black Widows,* and *Reservation Blues.* He has also received grants from the Lila Wallace–Reader's Digest Writers' Fund and the National Endowment for the Arts.

He recently wrote the screenplay for and coproduced *Smoke Signals,* a feature film produced by ShadowCatcher Entertainment and released by Miramax Films to great acclaim in 1998. It was the first feature film written, directed, and coproduced by American Indians to be nationally and internationally distributed.

About his work, Alexie writes: "I think my whole career has been about the effort to write accessible work, and by accessible, I mean I want my work to be understood and even enjoyed by the average twelve-year-old Indian kid growing up on some reservation or another.

"I recently had the experience of helping to create a movie that has been viewed by over a million people. Let me say that again. One million people. By my own estimates, I figure that ten thousand Indians have read one of my books. That's approximately one half of 1 percent of the total American Indian population. One year after our film premieres on home video, I would estimate that 90 percent of Indians will have seen *Smoke Signals.* I have come to understand that films are a populist art form, as opposed to the elitist art forms of poetry and literary fiction.

"So, what am I trying to say here? I want my poems and stories to resonate with the people, all of the people, and not just those who buy six or seven slim volumes of poetry a year. Hell, maybe stand-up comedy is the way to go. I'll just make sure the punch lines are in iambic pentameter."

Talvikki Ansel was born in 1962 and writes: "After receiving my MFA in creative writing from Indiana University, I was a Wallace Stegner Fellow in creative writing at Stanford University. *My Shining Archipelago* was selected by James Dickey for the Yale Younger Poets Award in 1996 and published by Yale University Press.

"My poems seem to begin with images or phrases, from here and there—observations, various jobs. 'You Don't Know What Happened When You Froze' started out with a few images and an anecdote I couldn't forget. 'Origin Charm Against Uncertain Injuries' I wrote after reading Francis Peabody Magoun's translation of the Finnish folk epic *The Kalevala*—I was drawn to the chanting quality and how the images were strung together."

Rick Barot was born in the Philippines in 1969. He attended Wesleyan University and the Writers' Workshop at the University of Iowa. His poems have been published in numerous periodicals, including the *Threepenny Review*, the *Yale Review*, and the *Paris Review*. He is currently a Wallace Stegner Fellow in poetry at Stanford University.

Barot writes: "I tend to think of my poems as boxes—think of Joseph Cornell's boxes—into which I put images. Of course story and music and feeling are in there too, but the image that can carry all three is what I'm after. An erotics of seeing, then, given language."

Paul Beatty was born in 1962 in Los Angeles and currently lives in New York City. He is the author of two books of poetry, *Joker, Joker, Deuce* and *Big Bank Take Little Bank*, both published by Penguin. His novel, *The White Boy Shuffle*, was published by Houghton Mifflin.

Erin Belieu was born in Omaha, Nebraska, in 1965. She has a BFA from the University of Nebraska, and master's degrees in English and writing from Ohio State University and Boston University. She has worked as a staff member for the Dukakis presidential campaign and as managing editor of *AGNI*, a literary journal, where she also acted as poetry editor for several years. She now teaches literature and creative writing at Kenyon College in Gambier, Ohio.

Belieu's first book, *Infanta* (Copper Canyon, 1995), was selected for publication by Hayden Carruth in the National Poetry Series and was chosen as one of the best books of poetry in 1995 by the National Book Critics' Circle and the *Washington Post Book World*. Her second collection of poetry, *One Above and One Below*, has just been published by Copper Canyon Press. Belieu's poetry has received the Rona Jaffe Foundation Prize and an Academy of American Poets Prize.

About her work, Belieu writes: "I've learned most about my own work through readers and critics who have sometimes made observations that, while initially startling to me, turned out to be very interesting and revealing (I find writing to be a mostly unconscious process—it's only later that I can sometimes see from where the impetus for a particular phrase or image came). One of the themes or recurring struggles in the poems seems to be trying to imagine a voice for those who don't always have a means of speaking or, more pointedly, of being heard.

Rafael Campo, MA, MD, teaches and practices general internal medicine at Harvard Medical School and Beth Israel Deaconess Medical Center in Boston. Born in 1964 to Cuban immigrant parents in Dover, New Jersey, he is a graduate of Amherst College, Boston University, and Harvard Medical School. He is the author of *The Other Man Was Me* (Arte Público Press, 1994), which won the 1993 National Poetry Series; *What the Body Told* (Duke University Press, 1996), which won the Lambda Literary Award for poetry; and *The Poetry of Healing: A Doctor's Education in Empathy, Identity, and Desire* (W. W. Norton, 1997), a collection of essays now available in paperback. His newest collection of poems, *Diva*, was recently published by Duke University Press and was written with the support of a John Simon Guggenheim Foundation Fellowship. His clinical practice at Beth Israel Deaconess Hospital in Boston serves primarily Latino, gay, lesbian, bisexual, and transgendered people, and people living with HIV. He is also actively involved in developing a medical humanities program at Harvard, which will bring together writers and artists who have explored the experience of illness in their work and medical students, residents, and hospital-based care providers, as well as their patients. He lives in Jamaica Plain, Massachusetts, with his life partner, Dr. Jorge Arroyo, and their red dobie named Ruby.

Nick Carbó writes: "I was born on October 10, 1964, in a barrio outside Legazpi City, Albay, in the Philippines, to a poor peasant family. My birth certificate says I was delivered by a 'hilot,' a midwife and spiritualist. She said I was destined to be a great orator or a loquacious person because of the presence of a mole above my upper lip. At six months of age, I was adopted by a Spanish couple of some means, and I began to speak the language that is closest to my heart. My father's family came from Catalonia, Spain, and I carry a Catalan surname. My mother's father came from Athens, Greece, so I also carry the name of Stilianopulos on my Spanish passport. I bear the weight of four cultures: Filipino, Spanish, Greek, and American, and this mix weaves in and out of my creative life, my poetry. And so does the presence of my American wife, the poet Denise Duhamel. What's the best thing about being married to another poet? All the glorious love poems we write to each other.

"I am the author of a book of poems, *El Grupo McDonald's* (Tia Chucha Press, 1995) and have edited *Returning a Borrowed Tongue: An Anthology of Filipino and Filipino American Poetry* (Coffee House Press, 1996). In 1997, I won a fellowship in poetry from the National Endowment for the Arts."

Joshua Clover won the Walt Whitman Award of the Academy of American Poets with his first book, *Madonna anno domini*. It was published in 1997 by Louisiana State University Press.

He writes that he was "born in San Francisco in 1962. Swerve of shore to bend of bay, etc.—back to San Francisco and environs, never in any one house for more than a year. Ashbery sez 'I tried each thing, only some were immortal and free'; I is the motion from each to each. That motion is identical to travel through the space of poems, wandering among buildings and along half-deserted streets, around sudden corners, permanent drift through the pure systems of language and money. These spaces are urban—they're cities and towns and suburbs. Poetics is urbanism; poems're never nature, they're handmade. Beauty and politics—the good shit—live in our interaction with such spaces: a police car on fire, the integuments filled with huge music, the promise *Under the paving stones, the beach!* painted slapdash on some wall. Poems must have all these, you must come upon each thing as if for the first time. Epictetus sez keep your eyes every day on loss, death, and exile. Duh. Meanwhile, one can do worse than to drift as one lost."

Nicole Cooley was born in 1966 and writes: "I grew up in New Orleans, Louisiana, and now live in New York City. My first book of poetry, *Resurrection*, won the 1995 Walt Whitman Award from the Academy of American Poets (chosen by Cynthia Macdonald) and was published by LSU Press in 1996. My novel *Judy Garland, Ginger Love* was just published by Harper Collins (Regan Books). I have received a National Endowment for the Arts grant in fiction and a 'Discovery'/ the *Nation* Prize in poetry. I am currently an assistant professor of English at Queens College CUNY.

"When I first began to write, as a child, I was shocked to discover a widely held belief about writing: poetry is supposed to be true, whereas fiction is all lies. So 'natural' we rarely question it, this difference might be restated as: poetry is autobiographical, fiction imagined. From the beginning, this dichotomy confused and troubled me, and it unsettles me still. In my own writing—both in my book of poetry and in my novel—I have worked to rethink the assumptions that surround the opposition of poetry vs. fiction. Thus, in my second book of poetry, I have challenged myself to explore the relation of poetry and history by re-imagining a historical event and by writing a sequence of poems that could be read like a novel, with repeating characters, stories, and scenes. This second book of poetry, *The Afflicted Girls*, focuses on the Salem witch trials of 1692. The poems examine what happened in Salem from the perspectives of a variety of people— the little girls who made accusations, the accused witches, members of families of men and women who were accused, even bystanders—and raise questions about the role of history, place, and identity in American culture."

Denise Duhamel was born in 1961 and is the author of ten books and chapbooks of poetry. Her most recent titles are *The Star-Spangled Banner* (winner of the Crab Orchard Award Series in Poetry, Southern Illinois University Press, 1999), *Exquisite Politics* (a collaborative work with Maureen Seaton, Tia Chucha Press, 1997), *Kinky* (Orchises Press, 1997), *Girl Soldier* (Garden Street Press, 1996), and *How the Sky Fell* (winner of the Pearl Editions chapbook contest, 1996). She has been included in three editions of *The Best American Poetry* and several other anthologies.

She writes: "I began to write books when I was about eight years old. I clearly remember taping them together and writing '59 cents' in a circle in the upper right hand corner of the cover. (I designed my picture books and novels to look like Golden Books.) I'd take my one-of-a-kind creations to Big Joe's supermarket and, when my mother wasn't looking, carefully place them in the magazine racks near *McCall's* or *Woman's Day.* When we returned the next week to shop, my books were always gone, which gave me a false sense of security, which actually lulled me into believing that I was being read."

Thomas Sayers Ellis was born in 1963 and raised in Washington, D.C. He is a founding member of The Dark Room Collective and a former coordinator of The Dark Room Reading Series. He studied with Seamus Heaney at Harvard and earned his MFA from Brown University under the tutelage of Michael S. Harper. His first collection, *The Good Junk*, appeared in the Graywolf/AGNI annual *Take Three* in 1995, and he has held residencies and fellowships at the MacDowell Colony, Yaddo, and the Fine Arts Work Center in Provincetown. He currently teaches in the English department at Case Western Reserve University and in the Bennington Writing Seminars.

About his work, Ellis writes: "I am interested in language, memory, thinking, feeling, history, and song (the center of marching), all at once. I try to make lines march across and down, both page and mouth. *The Good Junk* was, underneath everything else, about noise and its struggle to stay noise while confronting form, which is always asking it to become language, literature, and myth. Some noises resist and others give in. Depends on the poem or, to historicize it, where the march or protest is being held. Up South or Down North? In this way my poetics are definitely post–Civil Rights or post-Parks (as in Rosa). Writing I am marching. Fridays with Malcolm. Sundays with Martin. The poems in this anthology struggle there, resisting and negotiating whatever their contents and forms ask of them. Their meters are percussive. Groovallegiance. Feet. Feet. Feet. In fatigues and sync. Not singing. Some sanging. Song. Another way of putting it is to say that I work the way Mifune's character worked in Kurosawa's *Yojimbo.*"

Suzanne Gardinier was born in New Bedford, Massachusetts, in 1961 and grew up in Scituate, on the coast south of Boston. She received her BA from the University of Massachusetts at Amherst and her MFA from Columbia University.

Her first book, a long poem called *The New World*, was chosen by Lucille Clifton as the winner of the Associated Writing Programs Award in poetry in 1992, and she received a grant from the Lannan Foundation that same year. Her book of essays on poetry and politics, *A World That Will Hold All the People*, appeared as part of the Michigan Poets on Poetry Series in 1996. Her fiction has appeared in the *Village Voice*, the *Kenyon Review*, and the *American Voice*, and she is at work on a novel called *The Seventh Generation*. She teaches writing at Sarah Lawrence College and lives in Manhattan.

She writes: "Difficult as it is to remember now, we of the generation in this anthology were born in a country on the edge of revolution; my earliest memories—the demonstrations on the common, the television's blurts of war, Martin Luther King and Robert Kennedy lying in their blood with their visions for a whole future seeping over motel floors—are of one world seeming to die and another struggling to be born. Some of that change as perceived by a child was real, some turned back or illusory, but the taste and smell and ache of it trying to manifest itself were part of my first days and have never gone away. Poetry, in its insistence on truth, its collapse in the face of lies or illusions, was and remains for me the language of this incipient change, the language of revolution. The words are the branch trembling in my hand as I go looking for the river of it."

James Harms is the author of two collections of poetry, *Modern Ocean* and *The Joy Addict*, both from Carnegie-Mellon University Press. His poems have appeared in *Poetry*, *Ploughshares*, the *Missouri Review*, the *Kenyon Review*, and the *American Poetry Review*. He teaches at West Virginia University.

He writes: "A friend, another poet, once told me that she divided her acquaintances into two camps: those who could remember the assassination of John F. Kennedy and those who could not. She felt that this was the defining moment of the late twentieth century, or one of them, and that most of her close friends had been shaped by it, by the fact of the memory of the event or by the absence of that memory. Somehow, those of us who hadn't felt that sudden grief, that extraordinary and public sense of loss—somehow we were marked by the lack of this scar. An entire level of innocence was never ours to lose. It made us different somehow: not necessarily more cynical and not exactly less vulnerable. Different.

"I strikes me now that the watershed year 1960 (Kevin Prufer's cutoff year for this anthologyy) is significant in this regard: most people born since 1960 aren't likely to remember Kennedy's assassination. I don't, and I was born right in the middle of that year.

"I grew up in southern California—aware of all kinds of things I hadn't actually experienced—and tried hard not to be defined by Los Angeles (its endless surfaces, its ecstatic lifestyles) even as I was shaped by its landscape, by the way people moved across that landscape, a way of moving that felt strangely out-of-time, as if the lived moment were the only one, a perpetual present in the non-Buddhist sense. Consequently, it seems that memory is less important to me than invention (which must mean that L.A. has had its way with me) and that language is an instrument for me to enact a memory that is never fixed or certain. And yet, I've never wanted language to be the point, even as I've always feared that subject matter might become it. Perhaps it's because I've assumed from the start that subjects were provisional, that they could disappear at any moment. And maybe that's because I didn't witness their disappearance, just heard about it.

"Still, language is what comes between, as old-fashioned as that sounds, and I like the idea that I'm here to name and to see (not necessarily simultaneously). Charles Wright, a poet I would be pleased to consider an influence, wrote recently in a poem:

Journal and landscape
—Discredited form, discredited subject matter—
I tried to resuscitate both, bread and blood, making them whole again
Through language and strict attention—

This seems just about right. I would add that I like to hear people talk in poems (also old-fashioned), which is why I listen quite a bit to the New York poets (Ashbery, O'Hara, Schuyler, et al.). But I guess what I'm saying is that if we're a generation of poets who likes to sing instead of witness, it may not be that we're numb or cynical or bored or mistrustful. It may be that we just need to be given a little more time to sort through it all, to make sense of what we've lived through and what we've missed."

Allison Joseph writes: "I was born on January 18, 1967, in London, England, to Adella and Everest Joseph, immigrants from Jamaica and Grenada respectively. My family lived in England until I was three months old, then emigrated to Toronto, Canada. We moved to the Bronx when I was four. I graduated from the Bronx High School of Science in 1984, from Kenyon College in 1988, and from Indiana University in 1992. In 1992, my first book, titled *What Keeps Us Here*, was published by Ampersand Press of Roger Williams University. The book also won the John C. Zacharis First Book Prize from Emerson College and *Ploughshares*. My other awards include fellowships from the Bread Loaf and Sewanee Writers' Conferences, an Illinois Arts Council Artists' Fellowship in Poetry, and an Illinois Arts Council Literary Award. In 1997, my second and third books were published: *Soul Train*, from Carnegie-Mellon University Press, and *In Every Seam*, from the University of Pittsburgh Press. I currently teach at Southern Illinois University at Carbondale, where I also serve as poetry editor of *Crab Orchard Review*, a journal I helped to found. I see my role as poet, teacher, and editor as one that allows me to help make poetry more available and more accessible to those who seek it.

My poems touch on issues of family history, childhood, adolescence, race relations, and popular culture, but I strive to write poems that reach people of all backgrounds and circumstances."

Julia Kasdorf was born in 1962 in Mifflin County, which is one of Pennsylvania's oldest Amish and Amish Mennonite settlements. She grew up in a Mennonite home in Irwin, Pennsylvania, and attended Goshen College in northern Indiana before transferring to New York University, where she completed undergraduate studies. She studied creative writing with Sharon Olds, Galway Kinnell, and Yehuda Amichai in the NYU graduate program, and also completed a PhD in English education. Her dissertation is the first scholarly study of the cultural work of Joseph W. Yoder, an Amish musician and author from Mifflin County who lived early in the twentieth century.

With the acceptance of a first book, *Sleeping Preacher* (University of Pittsburgh Press, 1992) and the appearance of four of its poems in the *New Yorker* just prior to the book's publication, Julia Kasdorf became a representative poet of the Mennonite and Amish people. She writes that "the difficulty of this position has inspired reflection on the meanings of gender and ethnicity as they influence writing, and I am now working on a collection of essays on these subjects titled *Writing like a Mennonite*. Meanwhile, my recent collection of poems, *Eve's Striptease*, is more concerned with problems of the body, gender, sexuality, and pain."

After more than a dozen years in New York City, Julia Kasdorf moved in 1996 to south central Pennsylvania where she teaches at Messiah College.

Joy Katz was born in New Jersey in 1963. She was trained in industrial design but left her career in 1993 to concentrate on writing poetry. She received her MFA from Washington University in St. Louis and recently completed a Wallace Stegner Fellowship in poetry at Stanford University. She lives in Manhattan where she is a freelance writer and art director; her poetry has appeared in many literary magazines including *Quarterly West, Antioch Review,* and *Parnassus: Poetry in Review.* Her prose appears in the *New York Times Book Review, ArtForum, Parnassus: Poetry in Review, Mademoiselle,* and other publications.

She writes: "My poetry includes (but is not limited to) historical material, often finding its focus around situations where there is tension between beauty and terror. Sometimes there is a vision of a woman's presence in the situations. I am interested in the past (the discovery of the New World, Thomas Jefferson's life) but often wonder what is to be made of these obsessive yard goods. It is not enough for me to retell or recast the story; I want to place myself in the midst of it, 'muck around' in it through questions of voice (exploring the 'I' voice instead of using a persona or effaced narrator) and source material (using my own discourse in conjunction with direct quotes, like the ones in 'Taxonomy.')"

Timothy Liu was born in 1965 in San Jose, California, and is now an assistant professor of English at William Paterson University. He is the author of three books of poetry: *Vox Angelica* (Alice James, 1992, winner of the Norma Faber First Book Award), *Burnt Offerings* (Copper Canyon, 1995), and *Say Goodnight* (Copper Canyon, 1998). His poems have also appeared in *Grand Street*, the *Nation*, *New American Writing*, the *Paris Review*, *Poetry*, *Sulfur*, and elsewhere. His art reviews appear in *ARTnews*, *Art Papers*, and *New Art Examiner*.

He writes: "The intersection between the mainstream and the avant-garde continues to captivate the poets from my generation who interest me most. With one hand in the *Yale Review* and the other in *Talisman* is how I like to picture the conduit of poesy passing through my body. There are so many traditions, and yet we start where we start and go from there. I think of the poets Charles Wright and Gustaf Sobin, born in the same year, straddling the abyss. A confluence. As influences. Then I think of folks like David Shapiro and John Yau writing all that marvelous art criticism alongside their poems — that cross-fertilization ushered in by the New York School. How blessed we are to inhabit these times, this legacy."

Khaled Mattawa was born in Benghazi, Libya, in 1964 and emigrated to the U.S. in 1979. He is the author of a book of poems, *Ismailia Eclipse* (Sheep Meadow Press, 1995), and the translator of two books of Arabic poetry, Hatif Janabi's *Questions and Their Retinue* (University of Arkansas Press, 1996), and Fadhil Al-Azzawi's *In Every Well a Joseph Is Weeping* (Quarterly Review of Literature, 1997). His poems, essays, and translations have appeared in *Poetry*, the *Kenyon Review*, *Antioch Review*, *Michigan Quarterly Review*, *AGNI*, the *Paris Review*, *Pushcart Prize XXII*, and *The Best American Poetry*. He was the Alfred Hodder Fellow at Princeton University in 1995–1996 and was recently awarded a Guggenheim Fellowship and a grant from the National Endowment for the Arts. He has taught at Duke University, California State University-Northridge, and Indiana University, where he received an MFA in creative writing.

Jeffrey McDaniel was born in Center City, Philadelphia, in 1967. A graduate of Sarah Lawrence College and George Mason University, he is the author of *Alibi School* and *The Forgiveness Parade*, both published by Manic D Press. He has performed in over forty American cities, at venues such as the South by Southwest Music Festival, the Smithsonian Institute, and the Nuyorican Poets Café, and has been featured in *Ploughshares*, *The Best American Poetry 1994*, and on National Public Radio's *Talk of the Nation*. He lives in Los Angeles.

He writes: "While I don't consider myself a 'performance' poet or 'slam' poet per se, I have been influenced, in all sorts of ways, by my experiences in those communities. For instance, the poem 'Disasterology' was constructed at 3:00 A.M. on a hotel hallway floor in Asheville, North Carolina, during the 1994 National

Poetry Slam. I ripped my favorite lines out of five different poems and re-built them with the sole purpose of reading the new poem the next day at the 'competition.'"

Campbell McGrath was born in 1962 and is the author of four books of poetry: *Captialism, American Noise, Spring Comes to Chicago,* and *Road Atlas.* He is also the recipient of numerous prizes and fellowships, most recently a MacArthur Fellowship. He grew up in Washington, D.C., and has lived mostly in New York, Chicago, and Miami Beach, where he now resides with his wife and two sons.

He writes: "My writing focuses on American history, culture, and landscapes because they're what I know and care about most deeply and because America owes the world some explanations. I often cast my poems in prose and do not believe the perceived distinction between 'prose' and 'verse' is particularly meaningful or consequential. I admire the flexibility and omnivorousness of poetry as a medium for exploring and documenting the world. I listen to rock and roll music and plan to write a three-volume poetic investigation of Elvis Presley's afterlife in purgatory. My heroes include Woody Guthrie, Vincent Van Gogh, and Ludwig Wittgenstein. As much as I enjoy writing poems, I prefer watching *Scooby Doo* with my children on Cartoon Network to all other forms of human endeavor."

HeidiLynn Nilsson was born in 1974. During her childhood she lived in Washington, Louisiana, New Jersey, Virginia, and Michigan. She received her BA in English and religious studies from the University of Virginia and studied at Hollins College as a Rubins Writing Scholar. In 1998, she received her MFA in poetry writing from Washington University in St. Louis, where she won the Academy of American Poets Prize and the St. Louis Poetry Center's Open Competition. Her poems have appeared in *AGNI, TriQuarterly, Pleiades,* and other journals. She is currently finishing her first book while teaching in Baltimore, where she lives with her husband.

She writes: "Most of my poetry amounts to no more than a suspended meditation on what I consider to be the most unsettling aspect of universal human experience—namely, that we are given the opportunity (or compelled, as I sometimes see it) to take part in the task of creating ourselves. I am often overwhelmed by the many choices we face daily that will alter—or fix, even—our character. I find terrifying and fascinating how little I understand my own choices—how seldom my actions coincide with my convictions. Ultimately, I wish that God would cure either free will or evil."

Rick Noguchi was born in Los Angeles in 1967 and grew up surfing the beaches of southern California. He attended Santa Monica College and California State

University at Long Beach so he could surf before, between, after, and, quite often, during class. He writes that he spent more time studying the ocean than he did studying for school. He received his MFA in creative writing from Arizona State University in 1993. His book *The Ocean Inside Kenji Takezo* was chosen by Olga Broumas as winner of the 1995 Associated Writing Programs Award Series in poetry and was published by the University of Pittsburgh Press. *Publishers Weekly* selected the collection for its "Best Books of '96" list. Other publications include *The Wave He Caught*, which won the 1994 Pearl Editions chapbook contest.

While living in Arizona and studying poetry with Norman Dubie, Beckian Fritz Goldberg, and Alberto Rios, Noguchi continued to surf. "Nothing was different," he says. "The waves were the same. I surfed the same break. I rode the same surfboards. Only the drive to get there was a lot longer." For Noguchi, writing poetry and surfing are similar activities. Both require intense concentration, the ability to balance multiple moving objects at once, and the fortitude to wipe out now and then.

Noguchi currently writes in Los Angeles, where he lives with his wife, Deneen Jenks, and their daughter, Miyako Ann. He still surfs.

Barbara J. Orton writes: "I was born in North Carolina in 1969 to English parents; my brother and sister were English as well. My accent and idiom are consequently shifty, and my loyalties were complicated from the start. I attended Washington University in St. Louis, where I studied English and, later, writing. Since then, I've mainly worked variations on the theme of secretary, though I recall brief stints as a freelance proofreader, synagogue babysitter, and substitute dishwasher for a Hare Krishna restaurant. I write feverishly, sporadically, and never as often as I should.

"It's difficult to speak about one's poetry without stating the irrelevant or the obvious. In general terms, then: the things I value most in a poem are clarity, control, and emotional force. There are other qualities that I'm glad to find if I can—music, intellectual complexity, nuance—but, more than anything, I judge a poem by its bite."

Barbara J. Orton has published poetry in *Verse*, the *Literary Review*, *Pleiades*, the *Laurel Review*, and elsewhere. Her manuscript, *Stealing the Silver*, was a finalist for the Yale Younger Poets Prize. The *Literary Review* recently published her web chapbook in cooperation with Web Del Sol (www.webdelsol.com).

Alan Michael Parker was born in 1961 and has published poems in many journals, including *Antaeus*, *Boulevard*, *Field*, the *New Republic*, the *New Yorker*, the *Paris Review*, and *TriQuarterly*. His first book of poems, *Days like Prose*, was named a "Notable Book of 1997" by the National Book Critics Circle. His second collection, *The Vandals*, appeared in 1999 from BOA Editions. Parker is coeditor of *The Routledge Anthology of Cross-Gendered Verse*, as well as the editor for North America of *Who's Who in 20th Century World Poetry*. Since 1995, his book reviews have appeared regularly in the *New Yorker*.

Parker is an assistant professor of English at Davidson College in North Carolina, where he lives with his wife, the painter Felicia van Bork, and their son, Eli.

He has this to say about his poetry: "I have long been keenly interested in history. My second book, *The Vandals*, takes as its central dramatic figures the tribes of European invaders (of the same name). In my more recent work, I have begun to play with another set of characters from European history, the Penates, or household gods, that Aeneas brought with him when he founded Rome. Although my Vandals and Penates are decidedly contemporary and American, their skewed relationships to culture and to issues of individual spirituality seem oddly connected—I hope!—to those of their predecessors."

D. A. Powell was born in Albany, Georgia, in 1963. He studied at San Jose State University, Yuba College, Santa Rosa Junior College, and finally Sonoma State University, where he received his BA in English in 1991 and an MA in English two years later. He earned an MFA at the Iowa Writers' Workshop in 1996. His first book of poems, *Tea*, appeared from Wesleyan University Press in 1998. *Lunch*, his second book of poems, will be published by Wesleyan in the fall of 2000.

D. A. Powell writes: "I have not spent so much time writing as I have living, so I consider myself first the product of my life and the producer of my poetry only secondly. Or, to tell the truth, eleventhly or so (though being a poet has been climbing its way up my identity chart, especially since I've published a book and everything). I came to poetry the way I've come to many things in my life: not marching headlong into it like 'come-to-Jesus' time at a tent revival, but by and by in a rather incidental way, almost through a kind of inertia.

"To tell the truth, I never really liked poetry much when I was younger, and most of the time that I was writing it, I was making fun of it. I took poetry writing in school because it fulfilled a requirement, and I figured writing poems took a hell of lot less time than writing novels or essays.

"Or, to tell another truth, I discovered poetry through Dudley Randall's anthology *The Black Poets* and tried for a while to be a black poet, but with very little success.

"Both of these stories are somewhat correct. Anyway, at some point I must have crossed over that line, from writing poems that were mocking poetry or poems that were imitating poetry into the realm of actually writing poetry. And I'm not sure when that really occurred. I just know that my decision to go to the Iowa Writers' Workshop was an acknowledgment of my poetic destiny, and the decision was not made easily (in fact, I didn't show up the first time I was accepted and I think that pissed them off a bit). Anyway, I finally did go to Iowa, and I have not looked back with regret.

"A couple months before *Tea*, my first book, appeared, I was diagnosed with AIDS. And that has, of course, had to share the proverbial loft with my being a poet. Well, my life has been so blessed. Not necessarily easy, but definitely blessed. So I take this little burden as my portion of hardship. This is the situation I write from, around, through at present. Lots of poets have to search around for things to write about, against, or to. I have been absolved of that kind of problem.

"I have taken a lot from the world, so I would like to give something back. I can't build a museum or a hospital. I can't split an atom or solve complex mathematical problems. I can't lead, and really, I can't much follow either. But I guess I can write a poem, and that seems to mean something to someone else's life. And that's enough."

Claudia Rankine was born in 1963 and raised in Kingston, Jamaica, and New York City. She is the author of two books: *Nothing in Nature Is Private* (Cleveland State University Press, 1994) and *The End of the Alphabet* (Grove Press, 1998). Her work has appeared in many journals, including the *Southern Review*, *AGNI*, the *Kenyon Review*, and the anthology *On the Verge*. She teaches at Barnard College in New York.

Rankine writes: "These poems attempt to replicate the sensation of a sharp wind against the uncovered face, the open wound. These poems attempt to replicate the raw sensation of noon heat against the uncovered face, the open wound. Or, these poems become the gestures one makes within the deafening silence enveloping the body in sensation. Do words really mean anything? If you juxtapose them what do you get? Does anyone else see it? Do words have spirits? Can they haunt us? Can any haunting be communicated? I am curious about how one emotionally experiences experience. Nothing is before feeling, the feeling that draws one to a window or draws one in a window. I saw a thing and it made my heart leap. 'Heart leap' doesn't mean anything, but language might build the leap another way. To live is to feel. Poetry—can it replicate feeling? Is this what the lyric is?"

Matthew Rohrer writes: "I was born in Ann Arbor, Michigan, in 1970 and moved to Oklahoma when I was seven, though my heart remained in Michigan and I returned at age eighteen to find it just as I had left it. I attended the University of Michigan, where I won a Hopwood Award for poetry, and studied poetry—especially that of Ron Padgett, Ted Berrigan, and Alice Notley—with Ken Mikolowski. I received my MFA from the Iowa Writers' Workshop in 1994; I wasn't going to apply, but my mom made me do it. I studied with many great teachers there but was especially lucky to work with Jim Galvin. Then I moved to New York, where I am one of the poetry editors for *Fence* magazine.

"A *Hummock in the Malookas* was selected by Mary Oliver for the 1994 National Poetry Series and was published by W. W. Norton. Recently, I have written essays on James Tate and Tomaz Salamun. His work is very important to me and is, I think, some of the most powerful and profound poetry written in our time.

"There is a part of me that wants everything to be a logical system, and I am entertained by explaining things to myself in this way. I have also seen a wingèd snake on a path. What interests me is a poetry, like life, where both of these are true."

Ruth L. Schwartz was born in Geneva, New York, in 1962, and spent her childhood and early adulthood moving around the country. She left home at sixteen, received her BA from Wesleyan University and her MFA from the University of Michigan, then lived for thirteen years in the San Francisco Bay area. For many years, Schwartz made her living as an AIDS educator; she has also worked as a professional resumé writer. Recently, she relocated to Cleveland, Ohio, where she is now an assistant professor of creative writing at Cleveland State University.

Schwartz's first book, *Accordion Breathing and Dancing*, won the 1994 Associated Writing Programs Award and was published by the University of Pittsburgh Press in 1996. Her second manuscript, *Survival*, was a 1998 National Poetry Series finalist.

About her work, Schwartz writes: "The theme of the body and its transformations—through eros, illness, disability, and death—figure prominently in my work. My ten years in AIDS and cancer education and my close personal experience with kidney failure and transplantation have profoundly informed my writing; so has my visceral awareness of the violence and alienation so prevalent in urban American life at the close of the twentieth century. Still, my belief in joy—my inability to refrain from ecstatic reverie regarding the redemptive capabilities of sexuality and love—is at the core of my poetry.

"Mine is not a poetry of memory. My writing is almost invariably sparked by what I see, hear, feel around me *today*. Perhaps that's simply because my memory is poor, or perhaps it's my way of being faithful to the constantly evolving experience of life in a physical body."

Angela Shaw writes: "I was born in Denville, New Jersey, in 1967. When I was five, my family returned to my parents' native state of West Virginia, and there I grew up in the Appalachian Mountains. I graduated from Swarthmore College in 1990 and received an MFA from Cornell University in 1995. Since and in between, I've worked as a temp, a teacher, and an arts administrator. I'm grateful to have received a writing fellowship from the Fine Arts Work Center in Provincetown, a grant from the Constance Saltonstall Foundation for the Arts, and a

Jacob K. Javits Fellowship. My work has been anthologized in the 1994 and 1996 editions of *The Best American Poetry* and in *Pushcart Prize XXIII*.

"My desire to make poems—my love of the written and spoken word—has sprung up alongside a lifelong inclination toward silence. My work, then, tends to see female subjectivity as dual in nature, as being comprised of both a silent self and a speaking self. I'm most interested in the tension between these selves, in how women negotiate the complex relationship between their speech and their silences. In writing of this negotiation, I've become preoccupied with a woman's manipulations of her available resources—domestic spaces, clothing, religion, the body, and, ultimately, language itself."

Reginald Shepherd writes: "I was born in 1963 in New York City and raised in the Bronx. I received my BA from Bennington College, an MFA from Brown University, and a second MFA from the University of Iowa. Currently, I live in Ithica, New York, and am an assistant professor of English at Cornell University. My third book, *Wrong*, was recently published in 1999 by the University of Pittsburgh Press. Pittsburgh also published my second book, *Angel, Interrupted*, in 1996. My first book, *Some Are Drowning*, was published by the University of Pittsburgh Press in 1994, as winner of the 1993 Associated Writing Programs Award in Poetry. My poems have appeared in the *American Poetry Review*, the *Kenyon Review*, the *Nation*, the *Paris Review*, *Ploughshares*, *Poetry*, and many other journals, as well as the 1995 and 1996 editions of The Best American Poetry. I have received a 'Discovery'/the *Nation* Award, an NEA creative writing fellowship and an Illinois Arts Council poetry fellowship, among other awards and honors.

"The poems I love both seduce and baffle: their surfaces (aural, imagistic) invite one while refusing to be assimilated, denying the urge to master the poem rather than surrender to it as an experience. Growing up in the tenements and housing projects of the Bronx, I looked not for a reflection of my life but for an alternative to it, an affirmation of the possibility of otherness, the freedom to *not* be shackled by my self or my surroundings. T. S. Eliot was the first poet I ever read: his work frustrated me while enthralling me, a definition of fascination in persons as well as poems.

"The work of the poets to whom I have been most drawn resists the intelligence almost successfully, as Wallace Stevens said a poem must. Among those poets are, most abidingly, Stevens, Hart Crane, and the earlier, more crabbed, hermetic Auden; also Michael Anania, Ben Belitt, Paul Celan, Alvin Feinman, Jorie Graham, Ann Lauterbach, Medbh McGuckian, Michael Palmer, and John Peck. In their various ways, these are writers for whom the poem is something done, a new existence in the world, and not simply something said, mere commentary on what already is."

Larissa Szporluk was born in 1967 and has been writing poetry for ten years. Her first collection, *Dark Sky Question,* won the Barnard New Women Poets Prize and was published by Beacon Press in 1998. She is also the recipient of the Rona Jaffe Foundation Prize and has had poems published in *Michigan Quarterly Review,* the *Georgia Review, Grand Street,* and *Virginia Quarterly Review,* to name a few.

She writes: "A recent mother of two children, I just completed a second manuscript of poems in my rare quiet moments. The manuscript is tentatively entitled *Isolato* and deals with physical and psychic isolation from a variety of perspectives. For example, the title poem is empathetic towards the Earth and aims to be as close to an 'Earth' voice as possible.

"Strongly influenced by Emily Dickinson, Rainer Maria Rilke, Sylvia Plath, and Linda Gregg, I like to think of poetry as an almost physical vehicle, a means of transporting consciousness quickly and completely in the direction of the unknown."

Ann Townsend was born in Pittsburgh in 1962; she received her BA from Denison University and her MA and PhD from Ohio State University. Her first book of poems, *Dime Store Erotics,* won the 1997 Gerald Cable Poetry Prize and appeared in 1998. Other awards include the 'Discovery'/the *Nation* award, the Stanley Hanks Poetry Chapbook Prize, and a grant in fiction from the Ohio Arts Council.

Her poems, short stories, and critical essays have appeared in *Antioch Review,* the *Kenyon Review,* the *Nation,* the *North American Review,* the *Southern Review, TriQuarterly,* and elsewhere. She is a gardener and trained vocalist and currently lives in Granville, Ohio, where she is an associate professor of English at Denison University and where she directs the Jonathan R. Reynolds Young Writers Workshop.

She says this about her poetry: "My poems grow from my desire to make written language capture the sound effects of human passion and the drama of human interaction. Robert Frost called this the 'sound of sense.' I was trained as a singer, and that has affected how I think about the sounds my poems make. I'm highly conscious of the music inherent in the written word—from the single notes of phrases and thoughts to the formal construction of syntax and story. Because I'm also a fiction writer, many of my poems have a narrative center, a tale embedded like a nugget inside the song of the poem."

Natasha Trethewey was born in Gulfport, Mississippi, in 1966. She received her BA from the University of Georgia, her MA from Hollins College, and her MFA from the University of Massachusetts, where she is pursuing a PhD in American literature. Trethewey is the recipient of a grant from the National

Endowment for the Arts, and her poems have appeared in such journals as the *American Poetry Review, Callaloo,* the *Gettysburg Review,* the *North American Review,* and the *Southern Review.* Currently, she is an assistant professor of English at Auburn University.

About her work, Trethewey writes: "When I read James Baldwin's words, 'This is the only real concern of the artist: to recreate out of the disorder of life that order which is art,' I felt he was speaking directly to me. I began writing, then, because I had some things to make sense of—experiences from my past, as well as a collective past, that I needed to grapple with in order to understand. So memory exists for me, like the burden of history, as a necessary part of my work informing the way I understand things that are happening around me now. I am especially drawn to those things that suggest absence, and I am constantly attempting to investigate the reality beneath all things I've seen or known such as what's not said or written down yet or what's occurred outside the frame of a photograph. I write to discover what else is there, to uncover secrets."

Karen Volkman was born in Miami in 1967 and educated at New College, Syracuse University, and the University of Houston. Her first book of poems, *Crash's Law,* was selected for the National Poetry Series by Heather McHugh and published by W. W. Norton in 1996. She received a National Endowment for the Arts Fellowship in Poetry in 1993. Her poems have appeared in the *Paris Review,* the *American Poetry Review, Partisan Review, Colorado Review,* and *New American Writing* and have been chosen for the 1996 and 1997 editions of *The Best American Poetry.* A resident of Brooklyn, she has taught at New York University, the New School, and the Unterberg Poetry Center of the 92nd Street Y and has worked with Teachers & Writers Collaborative teaching poetry in the public schools. She spent the spring and summer of 1999 in residence at the Akademie Schloss Solitude in Stuttgart, Germany.

About her work, Volkman writes: "While *Crash's Law* took energy from the expressive possibilities of line length and stanza shape, my new book has at its center a series of untitled prose poems. American poetry's abiding suspicion of the prose poem heightened my sense of it as lawless, undefined space in which to develop a new lyric density. It is an amazingly malleable form, marrying the immediacy of image-centered poetry with the rhythmic resources of prose by playing metrical cadence against the looping line and flow of sentence and paragraph. Often addressed to an absent 'beloved,' an actual or metaphysical presence that compels their utterance, the poems are troubled into being by this loss and formally shaped by the loss of that fundamental poetic ordering principle, the line—thus reflecting both in form and content the absence of mediating force, a lack of rule that verges on emotional and lyric violence. An evolving construction throughout the book, the poems' speaker is not a singular, personal 'I' but a figure from a kind of atemporal folklore, buffeted by tenderness, terror, irony, or lust into elaborate evasions, exclamations, verbal hijinks, and lyric flights. I am deeply interested in the way such postures—which I see as more contingent, more violent and more immediate than the psychological investment inherent in the idea of persona—open out into new verbal and perceptual fields, mapping the mind's evolving positions in response to its variable and perilous encounters."

Rachel Wetzsteon writes: "I was born in New York City in 1967 and grew up there. After graduating from Stuyvesant High School, I received degrees from Yale, Johns Hopkins, and Columbia. My first book of poems, *The Other Stars*, won the 1993 National Poetry Series and was published by Penguin in 1994; my second collection, *Home and Away*, was published by Penguin in 1998. I have received a grant from the Ingram Merrill Foundation, as well as fellowships to the Bread Loaf, Sewanee, and Wesleyan Writers' Conferences and residencies at MacDowell and Yaddo. I currently teach writing and literature at Barnard and the Unterberg Poetry Center of the 92nd Street Y, and am hard at work on a new book of poems.

"I hope none of the five poems included here needs *too* much explaining, but perhaps a little commentary is in order. 'Drinks in the Town Square' and 'Urban Gallery' were written around the same time and demonstrate, I think, my love of writing about cities and the often tumultuous situations that unfold in them. I should probably also point out that 'Urban Gallery' is the first poem in *The Other Stars* and introduces many of the book's main preoccupations. I think 'Poem for a New Year' is pretty self-explanatory. The other two poems are about writing. I wrote 'A Rival' when I was still in college, and used the poem as a chance to brood over the choice any young writer needs to make between the two kinds of writing personified by the main characters of the poem: while one of them blithely drops names and imitates her elders, the other wanders through cold forests, refusing to assimilate herself so easily to a ready-made tradition. 'The Late Show' is a polemic against a kind of poetry that resists being too ambitious in its imaginative or thematic reach, since everything important has already been said, and 'never getting there' is, for good or ill, the human condition. But these assumptions can result, I argue, in poems so cerebral and self-reflexive (qualities represented by the 'hand-held mirror') that the real world ('the things you saw in the rising tide') gets obscured. I wrote the poem in order to explore both the strengths and the weaknesses of this kind of poetry."

Greg Williamson writes: "I was born in 1964 and grew up in Nashville, Tennessee. After graduating from Vanderbilt University, I received an MA in English literature from the University of Wisconsin, and an MA in writing from Johns Hopkins University, where I've been teaching ever since.

"My first book, *The Silent Partner,* won the 1995 Nicholas Roerich Prize for Poetry and was published by Story Line Press. Individual poems have appeared in the *Yale Review,* the *New Republic,* *Poetry,* the *Paris Review,* AGNI, *Southwest Review,* the *Sewanee Review,* *Partisan Review,* and others. In 1998, 'The Dark Days' was given the Smartt Family Foundation Award for the 'best poem in the *Yale Review* during the preceding year' and was also included in *The Best American Poetry 1998* anthology. That fall, I received a Whiting Writer's Award from the Whiting Foundation.

"'Appalachian Trees Encircled by Police Tape' is from a collection of twenty-six poems called *Double Exposures.* You see, I'm looking through the prints of a roll of film, and they're all exposed twice. In each of the two sets of lines in a poem, I try to describe or explain or comment upon one of the exposures. My hope is that someone would read the right side first, then the left, then read them together, and that the two exposures would mesh into one in unexpected ways, as they do in pictures.

"This particular poem considers the origins of artistic 'inspiration' (a 'breathing into'). Tradition sometimes places the origin outside the artist: 'I was inspired by the scene or events or the muse.' Sometimes it places it within the artist: 'I was inspired by my feelings or thoughts or the muse.' In this poem, both of those places would appear to be poisoned. What, then, will our art look like?"

Max Winter was born in 1970 and writes: "My poems have appeared or are forthcoming in the *Paris Review,* the *New Republic,* *Boulevard,* and *The Prose Poem: An International Journal.* I have published reviews in *Boston Review,* the *Boston Book Review,* the *San Francisco Review,* the *New York Times Book Review,* and elsewhere. I am currently the associate editor of *Fence* and an on-staff reviewer for *Publishers Weekly.* I hold a BA in English from Columbia University, an MA in English from Washington University, and an MFA from the University of Iowa Writers' Workshop.

"The artistic values most important to me are a simultaneous catholicity of taste and a resistance to pre-established platforms or antiplatforms. The voice that develops in a writer's work will by necessity be one that grows out of influence, but need poetry be a set of carefully orchestrated echoes? I also like to think that there is no poetry without narrative (two parts arc, one part arch); I feel a need to give readers a reason to continue reading—and by extension, to continue living. And yet this present cannot be given on command. And it also cannot be announced within the poem, or the thrill is gone. Have I made myself clear? I only ask because clarity is so important; why bother to bring yourself to the page if your main purpose is to push yourself away from it through a display of educated uncertainty? Which is not to bad-mouth ambiguity; as a step, it's wonderful, but as an end, it's endless—and not particularly original. Which reminds me that I like to write things that have never been written and will never be written again—not too outlandish a goal, eh? And the things that find their way onto the page as 'new,' for me, are seamless images of my childhood, which may well have been yesterday. And these images are neither casual nor disparate but honest: true to me and, maybe, to you, in some small, persistent way."

Sam Witt was born in 1970 in Wimbledon, England, and was educated at the University of Virginia and the University of Iowa. His poems appear in *Volt*, the *Georgia Review*, *Virginia Quarterly Review*, *Poetry Northwest*, and elsewhere. He now lives in San Francisco and works as a freelance writer.

"Instead of writing a narrative, autobiographical blurb, I think I'll try to convey the sense of wonder poetry has given me by repeating passages I've written down in my journal, late at night:

> Poetry is a ceaseless craving for transformation, movement, change, free-dom . . . the joy of misusing words with all its concomitant sensations—rejuvenation, humility, the awkwardness of passion . . . it must live in a different language from what experience lives in . . . the trace of experi-ence . . . a nonlinear impulse . . . not the thing, but a representation of where the thing was, a reverse thing, in order to let its other-selves shine through . . .

"In the end, a few fragments are the best I can do. I write poetry because I can and because I care about it more than anything else. Beyond that, I think I'll let the poems speak for themselves."

Mark Wunderlich was born in 1968 in Winona, Minnesota, and grew up in rural Fountain City, Wisconsin. He was educated at the University of Wisconsin, Concordia College's Institute for German Studies, and Columbia University. He has lived for six years in New York City, where he worked as an arts administrator. From 1995 to 1996, he served as director of the University of Arizona Poetry Center in Tucson, and now lives in San Francisco.

Wunderlich's first book, *The Anchorage*, was published by the University of Massachusetts Press in 1999. He has published poems in the *Yale Review*, the *Paris Review*, *Poetry*, *Boston Review*, *Southwest Review*, *Chelsea*, and many other journals and anthologies. His awards and honors include a Wallace Stegner Fel-lowship from Stanford University, a fellowship from the Fine Arts Work Center in Provincetown, the Writers@Work Poetry Award, and an Arts Administration Fellowship from the literature program at the National Endowment for the Arts.

Kevin Young was born in 1970 and moved six times before he was ten years old, when he and his family settled in Topeka, Kansas—birthplace of both the poet

Gwendolyn Brooks and the painter Aaron Douglas and once childhood home of Langston Hughes.

Young attended Harvard University as an undergraduate, where he won the Academy of American Poets Prize. He went on to a Stegner Fellowship in Poetry from Stanford and an MFA from Brown University. Currently an assistant professor of English and African American studies at the University of Georgia, Young teaches poetry and film studies.

Young's first book, *Most Way Home*, won the National Poetry Series and the John C. Zacharis First Book Prize from *Ploughshares*; William Morrow published it in 1995. As the title implies, the book considers questions of home, displacement, and exile—and ultimately the African American vernacular.

Young writes that 'Campbell's Black Bean Soup' is the first poem in a book-length series based on the work of the late artist Jean-Michel Basquiat—who inspired Young to "move beyond narrative and further into the vernaculars of popular black culture, visiting the boxing ring, the bar, the barrio, and the electronic babysitter. Using Basquiat as a bass line, the poems riff off black 'figures' from Jack Johnson to Richard Pryor, Billie Holiday to Grace Jones—often in the same poem—in order to celebrate and connect black genius in all its forms and too-often tragic outcomes."

Poems from this collection, entitled *To Repel Ghosts*, have appeared in the *New Yorker*, the *Kenyon Review*, *DoubleTake*, *Grand Street*, *Crab Orchard Review*, and *Callalloo*, among other journals. Several poems were featured in the catalog and traveling exhibition *Two Cents*, installed in the galleries by Young alongside Basquiat's works-on-paper.

Young is currently completing a book of blues poems and editing *Giant Steps: The New Generation of African-American Writers*, an anthology of young black writers to be published by Morrow.

Kevin Prufer was born in 1969, grew up in Cleveland, Ohio, and is now an associate professor in the creative writing program at Central Missouri State University. His first collection of poetry, *Strange Wood*, won the Winthrop Poetry Series and appeared in 1998. He has other poems in the *Southern Review, Boulevard, Prairie Schooner, TriQuarterly, Antioch Review,* and elsewhere. He coedits *Pleiades: A Journal of New Writing.*